IRISH NEW YORK

BY LESLIE JENKINS AND BOB SWACKER

UNIVERSE

page 1: postcard: Erin go bragh!

page 2: Mrs. Thomas McKessy, of Limerick, upon arrival on the SS *Aurania*. She is joining her husband who came with ten of her family of twenty-one children, March 16, 1926.

page 3: St. Patrick's Cathedral, 1878. endpapers: map of Irish Manhattan by Andrew Keating

First published in the United States of America in 2006 by

UNIVERSE PUBLISHING
A Division of Rizzoli International Publications, Inc.
300 Park Avenue South
New York, NY 10010
www.rizzoliusa.com

Copyright © Leslie Jenkins and Bob Swacker

2006 2007 2008 2009 / 10 9 8 7 6 5 4 3 2 1
ISBN-10: 0-7893-1379-0
ISBN-13: 9-780789-313799
Library of Congress Control Number: 2005909604
Editor: Ellen Cohen
Designed by Paul Kepple @ Headcase Design
www.headcasedesign.com

Printed in Hong Kong

Dedicated to the Famine Irish and 1916

ACKNOWLEDGMENTS

The authors gratefully acknowledge the professional contributions of archivists and librarians Patrick McNamara of the Diocese of Brooklyn Archives, Barry Moreno of the National Park Service at Ellis Island, William Cobert and Scott Kelly of the American Irish Historical Society, Faye Haun and Melanie Bower of the Museum of the City of New York, Steve Taylor of Vassar College, Karen Broderick, Elizabeth Ferber, photographer James Casserly, and artists Dave McCutcheon, Andrew Keating, and Greg de la Haba. Special thanks to Ellen Cohen, Leslie Falk, and David McCormick.

CONTENTS

THE IRISH CONTRIBUTIONS

You're *if you are Irish* My Darlint.

The Irish steadily immigrated to New York City from the earliest Dutch and British colonial periods and by 1830 they represented almost one-fifth of the city's residents. From 1830 until 1845, Ireland's population continued to swell until An Gorta Mór, which translates from Gaelic as "The Great Hunger." Starving tenant farmers fled their homeland between 1845 and 1852 as the famine spread across Ireland, leaving them without sustenance. By the completion of St. Patrick's Cathedral in 1859, the Irish emigration surge had nearly doubled those already living in New York City. The Irish flowed into the New York seaport in boatloads, bringing an influx of more than 848,000 during the five-year period from 1847 to 1851.

Although the Irish no longer define New York's cultural identity, in many ways they have molded New York in their image. On St. Patrick's Day, each March 17th, New York City reverts to its Irish halcyon days. Unlike the St. Patrick's Day parades of yore, the faces of New York's police and firefighters are no longer all pale rosy-cheeked Irish, but now represent the vast diversity of the city. Still, legions of uniformed officers march up Fifth Avenue each year on the religious holiday, honoring St. Patrick. For many, it is a day New Yorkers hold dear as the celebration of their city's Irish heritage.

And what a heritage it is. The Irish brought a literate culture, improving America through words in books, poems, plays, and

(Above) Postcard. (Opposite) In the late nineteenth century, thousands of young Irish colleens came from Ireland straight into high demand positions as domestics.

songs. It dominated the city's political, economic, and social life from the mid-nineteenth century through the first quarter of the twentieth. The zealous religious and political Irish leadership also brought about vast social reforms for the poor and needy.

The story begins with the steady tide of Irish immigration from colonial times to the great surge during the potato famine. It ends with the Irish now a part of a greater immigration story, the history of New York City as a place where many groups seek refuge and new opportunities. The Irish saga does not end with the twentieth century but continues into the next millennium, as Irish New Yorkers continue to represent a large part of the spirit and voice of the Big Apple.

Chapter One

AN GORTA MÓR: THE GREAT HUNGER

The Irish came early and late to New York City with a huge spike in immigration as a result of the Potato Famine Diaspora. The years from 1845 to 1850, the famine among the tenant farmers of Ireland, known as An Gorta Mór, unleashed a torrential flood of Irish emigrants. Many arrived in America's largest port and stayed in the city, lacking funds to travel further. In 1847, approximately forty immigrant-laden ships were arriving at the city docks each week. Later in the 1920s, the 1950s and the 1980s mini-immigration peaks once again occurred.

In a massive grassroots relief effort sparked by the Potato Famine, Irish Americans funded as many as half of the passage tickets of the starving Irish refugees. The walls surrounding the famine memorial at Battery Park City are covered with a list of the contributors to this relief effort and a haunting recording recalls the terrible story. The tenant farmers emigrated to avoid death from starvation. Those who knew they would never see Éire again referred to immigration to America as "the American Wake." They came to escape English oppression and the abject poverty and disease born of such oppression, but their love for Ireland never left them.

The passage took anywhere from one to three months, depending on the weather. Below-deck steerage accommodations were communal and overcrowded. On some of the ships, popular-

(Above) The Irish Hunger Memorial located in Battery Park City at the corner of Vesey Street and North End Avenue in lower Manhattan commemorates the Diaspora of Ireland's tired, hungry, huddled masses during the famine. (Opposite) Mrs. Bridget Casey of Cork, Ireland, with her nine children, arriving on the SS *Berlin* on December 2, 1929. They are en route to Bridgeport, Conn., where their father is with two other children. The second eldest child was left in Ireland having failed to pass the Immigration Department test.

ly known as "Coffin Ships," as many as a third of the steerage passengers died.

Most of the emigrants had left the Irish port towns in the barely seaworthy ships with nothing but the clothes on their backs, a few cooking items, bedding, and a small amount of cash. When they disembarked in Manhattan, helpful fraternal and religious groups assisted some, but predatory pickpockets, con artists, and thieves met many more. They were steered into overpriced boarding houses, put into the service of unscrupulous employment agents, robbed of what little they had, or sold counterfeit train tickets.

At the crest of Irish immigration, the gateway to the largest port in North America was not Ellis Island, but Castle Garden. Castle Garden, opened in 1855, was run not by the federal government but by the state government. It was initially located on an islet 100 yards off the Battery at the southern tip of Manhattan and was connected to the shore by a narrow wooden walkway. It was the first immigration center to be operated by any government. Two million immigrants from Ireland passed through Castle Garden. Eventually landfill connected it to the shore. Renamed for Governor Clinton, it is now called Castle Clinton; its shell is still at the foot of Manhattan in Battery Park.

The federal immigration facility, Ellis Island, was not operational until 1892. The first immigrant to pass through Ellis Island was a fifteen-year-old Irish lass, Annie Moore, who, with her two younger brothers, were joining their parents, who had immigrated earlier. Upon their arrival in New York, the Irish refugees from the famine in Ireland were met with vicious persecution. Anti-Catholic and anti-Irish epithets were common. The Irish became even more clannish in reaction, banding together through Catholic and fraternal organizations. The wealthy Protestants cleaved to the Republican Party, and the Catholics, banding together in opposition, became Democrats.

(Above) The haunting image of Bridget O'Donnel and her two children is one of the most striking images of the Famine.

The Irish-Americans and nativists, who were generally American-born of English descent, often fought in pitched street battles, as depicted in the 2002 movie, *The Gangs of New York*. The Five Points area became a battleground. The Irish lived there in abject poverty, an underclass plagued by overcrowding, ignorance, unemployment, alcoholism, violence, prostitution, child abandonment, gang warfare, and street crime. Their appalling poverty and crime born of absolute desperation fed the backlash of bigotry and anti-Catholic sentiment.

By the mid-1800s, those immigrants who survived the initial induction into urban American life became reverential American patriots, as the Irish began to garner paying jobs and political favors. To the refugees from the Emerald Isle, the United States became the land of plenty, and even the rookeries and tenements of the crowded Manhattan slums were better than starvation in the hovels of Ireland. As their numbers grew, the Irish rose to prominence in all walks of life.

In 1850, during the Potato Famine, Orestes Brown, a celebrated convert to Catholicism, stated: "Out of these narrow lanes, dirty streets, damp cellars, and suffocating garrets, will come forth some of the noblest sons of our country, whom she will delight to own and honor." A little more than a century later, John Fitzgerald Kennedy, the first Irish Catholic American president, was in the White House.

(Above) Painting by Samuel B. Waugh (detail) of the arrival of a ship bearing Irish immigrants at the Battery adjacent to Castle Garden.

The close of 1850 marked the peak of Irish immigration to New York City and the end of The Great Hunger in Ireland. According to census reports, one out of every four residents of the city was Irish-born or of Irish heritage. For more than fifty years, from 1820 through 1870, Ireland was the biggest source of immigrants to the United States. Irish culture, both high and low, permeated New York City's social, political, economic, and religious life.

The notorious Five Points neighborhood (now Chinatown and Foley Square) in the Sixth Ward was named for the five points formed by the intersections of Anthony (now Worth), Little Water, Orange (now Baxter), and Mulberry Streets, which met at a small iron-fenced park known as Paradise Square. Both the squalid Fourth Ward and the teeming Sixth Ward were home to the most destitute of the poverty-stricken famine immigrants. With poverty comes crime, and in 1850 Five Points accounted for 60 percent of the city's criminal offenses.

Originally, city planners built the Five Points neighborhood on landfill over a cesspool called the Collect Pond. Due to the

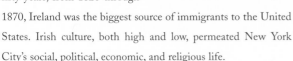

(Above) *Below Decks* by Rodney Charman depicting Irish famine immigrants below decks on an immigrant laden ship.
(Opposite) *Famine Immigrants Arriving at the South Street Seaport Docks in Lower Manhattan* by Rodney Charman.

overcrowded unsanitary conditions of the area, one out of every seventeen residents in Five Points died in 1854. During the 1850s, Five Points was second only to Dublin in the number of its Irish denizens, and conditions of overpopulation were desperate. Diseases of human crowding and overuse, such as cholera, typhus, and tuberculosis, took their toll among all age groups and the infant mortality rate among Irish New York families was a staggering 80 percent.

Due in large part to the slum conditions that defined the immigrants, anti-Catholic and anti-Irish sentiment, as shamelessly exhibited in Thomas Nast's cartoons for *Harper's Weekly*, was flagrant. The press portrayed the Irish as lazy, degenerate, ignorant, violent, apelike drunkards who were themselves responsible for their plight. In the two decades before the Civil War, more than half the people arrested in New York City were Irish. Law enforcers called the police vans they used to round up transgressors "paddy wagons" ("Paddy" is the nickname for "Patrick," the name of the Patron Saint of Ireland and a common Irish

(Opposite) Painting by Samuel B. Waugh of the arrival of a ship bearing Irish immigrants at the Battery adjacent to Castle Garden.

TO OUR STARVING POOR—IF YOU WANT RELIEF, GO TO IRELAND.

given name), termed a street fight a "Donnybrook" (an Irish town), and referred to iron bars on ground-floor residential windows as "Irish bars."

However, even Five Points gradually evolved as the Irish found work through Tammany Hall under the stewardship of ward leaders and in many other burgeoning professions throughout the flourishing economy. By 1880 Five Points was home to only 10 percent of the city's total crime. Whereas two-thirds of the Five Points population had been illiterate in 1850, only 10 percent could not read by 1890. By the end of the nineteenth century, drug use and alcoholism declined proportionally as well. For the most part, gone were the days when "No Irish Need Apply."

Geographically, the Irish began to spread throughout the city as they became gainfully employed. They began to populate the Lower East Side, South of Houston (SoHo), and Greenwich Village. Later the Irish established communities in Queens and Brooklyn, such as in Astoria, Long Island City, Williamsburg, Greenpoint, Bushwick, and South Brooklyn. Staten Island's Irish enclave surrounded Saint Mary's Church in Rosebank. Despite an inauspicious start, the vast majority of Irish immi-

(Above) An 1874 wood engraving of immigrants leaving Queenstown (Cobh) for New York.
(Opposite) A political cartoon published in *Puck* magazine in 1880 protesting the export of monies to Ireland for relief efforts.

grants proved themselves to be both law-abiding and industrious citizens, taking advantage of economic opportunities when available. There were certainly more chances for economic gain and stability as the city's population doubled in the years from 1850 to 1880 from 500,000 to 1.1 million residents.

The City of New York, following London's example, passed the Municipal Police Act in 1845 and established a full-time professional police force. The ranks of New York's finest swelled with Irish immigrants. The city organized the Metropolitan Fire Department, a corps of paid professionals, in 1865 to replace the largely Irish-dominated volunteer companies. However, despite the disbanding of the volunteer companies, the Irish continued to dominate the firefighting forces through the patronage system that assured Irish control of the Fire Department as well.

Because Irish immigrants had started to climb both economic and social ladders earlier than the twentieth-century Ellis Island arrivals, they enjoyed the benefits of the middle class that much sooner.

The New York City Irish, with their clannish ways, steadfastly maintained a strong cultural identity through their fraternal organizations, Irish county affiliations, religious groups, and artistic traditions. In Ireland, persecution by the English caused them to band together. After immigration, the same anti-Irish and anti-Catholic sentiments further enforced their separatist stance. In America, their primary opposition was the American Republic Party, commonly called the "Know Nothings" because, if asked about their party, they answered, "I know nothing." The Know Nothings wanted America to remain in the hands of those with English

(Above) "Outward Bound," 1850s (Opposite) A photo by Jacob Riis of Mullen's Alley, where the Irish street urchins display their city-wise adaptation to urban life.

ancestry. In reaction to the nativists, the Irish found their support in Tammany Hall. They were the most powerful ethnic voting block and remained so for a century.

The Irish never wanted to leave Ireland. They were driven out by English policies, and only the hardy survived to continue their fight against the same problems born of poverty, disease, unemployment, and starvation. Many felt that the only difference between their situation in Ireland and America was an agrarian setting versus an urban one. Their fervor for American opportunities was eclipsed only by their continued cultural allegiance to Ireland.

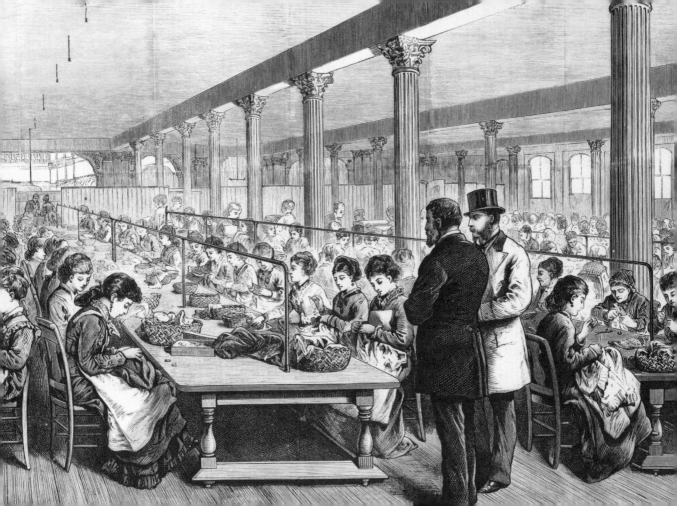

Of all the New York City immigrant groups, the Irish represented the largest block of early arrivals in the nineteenth century. This provided a distinct advantage when unskilled labor was needed to build the city as it advanced northward at a dizzying

City Irish, who had a lock on City Hall and enjoyed the benefits of its patronage and nepotism.

Most of the new Irish immigrants poured into the First, Fourth, and Sixth Wards with some spread into the adjacent parts of the Fourteenth Ward.

pace. In the last half of the nineteenth century, New York City stretched its geographic limits uptown by several streets each year. By 1850, the city had expanded to 42nd Street, and by 1860, to 60th Street. As the city grew, civil service jobs increased exponentially under Tammany Hall patronage, and many of the positions went to the Irish. These were the halcyon days for the New York

A listing of typical occupations for Irishmen during the early part of the nineteenth century included laborers, bottling porters, waiters, riggers, grocers, boot makers, sail makers, tailors, painters, tanners, machine makers, fruit sellers, slaughterers and other various low-end trades. By 1820, the Five Points neighborhood was marked by an absence of city services and was overpopulated with

(Above) *Milkman* by John O'Connell (Opposite) The sewing room at A. T. Stewart's Department Store in 1875, where thousands of young Irish women were employed. This depiction is of the "uptown" store after it moved from Broadway and Chambers to ninth and tenth Streets and between Broadway and Fourth Avenue.

some of the city's poorest residents. Most of the denizens were newly arrived immigrants and a small group of African Americans. By 1819, Five Points was 25 percent Irish. Five Points had a reputation for being the worst slum in the city, although the Fourth Ward to the east rivaled its reputation with, among other things, boggy streets full of water.

By the 1820s, the earlier Irish arrivals had begun their ascent to the middle class and had moved uptown to Greenwich Village. The wealthier upper classes had begun to move further north on the island, thus vacating the lower areas and creating available housing. Spaces were not left empty for long, especially once famine victims began arriving in droves. By 1855, the Irish comprised 50 percent of the slums in the First, Fourth, and Sixth wards. The reason for this concentration of Irish immigrants was simple as these wards

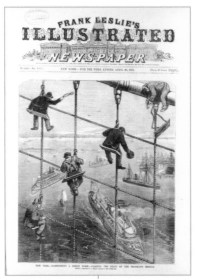

offered the lowest rents and the largest number of unskilled labor jobs. The new arrivals had to pay their dues at the low end of the economic scale before beginning their ascent.

The influx of Famine Irish created a pool of workers unskilled in marketable trades. The jobs available to them were generally menial and barely offered a subsistence wage. Irishmen arriving after the great tragedy lacked skills due to the legacy of the Penal Laws in Ireland, which forbade them from entering into trades in their own country. As a direct consequence, the mid-nineteenth-century immigrants could only work in a variety of unskilled jobs as common laborers. A few intrepid and savvy individuals turned into entrepreneurs and became, among other things, grocers, fishmongers, junk dealers, booksellers, and saloonkeepers. However, the majority of immigrants at this time

(Above) The construction crew for the East River Bridge, later renamed the "Brooklyn Bridge," was predominately of Irish descent. Here laborers are shown tightening the cables on the bridge, a dangerous job undertaken by Irish immigrants.

1.—ENTRANCE TO THE SUPPLY-SHAFT OF THE CAISSON.

2.—MOUTH OF SUPPLY-SHAFT OF THE CAISSON.

3.—DRILLING THE ROCK AT THE EDGE OF THE CAISSON.

4.—DOOR THROUGH PARTITION, SHOWING DIFFERENT APARTMENTS IN THE CAISSON.

5.—FEEDING THE BUCKET OF THE WATER-SHAFT IN THE CAISSON.

6.—WORKMEN SAWING TIMBER FOR WEDGES.

gravitated toward work offered to them by Irish fraternal groups. Within these organizations they found a shared cultural identity and camaraderie. Capitalizing on their clannishness, the Irish elected politicians to Tammany Hall who could directly aid them in certain areas of employment. The politicians gave them, in kind, civil service jobs and positions in the city's burgeoning construction industry. Steering projects towards contractors who were well connected politically was one such method of creating livelihoods for the newest wave of Irish citizens in New York City.

In early New York, the Common Council, and later its successor, the City Council, had the power to issue licenses for various occupations, for example a carting license. Carting was a trade with few start-up costs and little overhead, making it an attractive choice for an ambitious immigrant. Not surprisingly, the carting industry became the earliest example of the Irish exercising their collective political muscle.

Despite the fact that all a person needed to run a moderately successful carting business was a horse, cart and harness, and an

(Opposite) Jobs by Irish Americans during the construction of the East River Bridge (Brooklyn Bridge).

empty lot in which to stable the horse and keep the cart, the city refused to issue carting licenses to the Irish until the War of 1812. Preceding the war, a group of native-born citizens appealed to the City Council to ban non-native-born residents from obtaining carting licenses. In response to this economic and political bid, the City Council limited the cargo of Irish carters to dirt. In spite of this act, the ever-persistent and eager Irish immigrants monopolized the carting trade by the 1820s. In response to their dominance in the trade, the heavily Irish Sixth Ward became known as the "Cartman's Ward." The Irish dominated the trade well into the nineteenth century and gradually controlled all the licenses for the service.

Now that they commanded one major trade in the city, the Irish turned their attention to gaining licenses in other lucrative commercial areas. Their burgeoning political power helped the Irish achieve access to such industries as furniture, second-hand clothing, rag dealing, and pawn brokering. Some entered into business without a license, and many of these illegitimate peddlers lined Orange Street in 1850. Gradually, however, the Irish made inroads even into the licensed professions, gaining both commercial and cultural standing in New York City. Groups such as The Loco Foco (a radical spur of the Democrats) aided the Irish in their attempts to rise in society by supporting legislation that would ensure equal access to licenses for all.

Irish children were not exempt from finding work to help support themselves, families, and relatives in the old country. Seeking whatever low-level, unskilled labor they could find, children generally looked to the street for work. Irish "corn girls" peddled corn, flower girls sold flowers, young

STREET SWEEPER

(Above and Opposite) Irish street sweeper from *Sunshine and Shadow in New York* by Matthew Hale Smith, first published in 1868.
The two buildings are intended to be in sharp contrast and are architectural representations both ends of the New York Irish social spectrum.
On the top is the mansion of A. T. Stewart, Irish proprietor of the first department store in New York.

children swept garbage-strewn alleys, and newspaper and bootblack boys plied their trades to hurried customers.

Despite progress, "nativists" still dominated the skilled trades, shunning newcomers and discouraging the Irish from making inroads into the licensed industries. In response to this exclusion, Irishmen turned to more clannish types of professions, becoming policemen, firemen, and contractors. In these fields the pleasant camaraderie with fellow countrymen could take the place of family life for many young men, who chose to delay marriage until, among other reasons, they felt more secure financially. By 1855, 27 percent of the New York City police force consisted of men of Irish decent.

In A. E. Costello's *History of the New York Police*, published in 1885, he states, "It's safe to say that nearly every appointment is made through personal or political influence. Those who cavil at this should remember that this almost invariably secures for the Department men who have lived long enough in this city to know it, for politicians and friends of Police Commissioners are not disposed to interest themselves in strangers."

An Irishman with an illustrious career, Thomas Byrnes became head of the Detective Bureau in 1883 and initiated the now famous "third degree." The Irish-born Inspector Byrnes came to America as a small child and rose through the police ranks at a rapid clip:

patrolman in 1863, roundsman in 1868, sergeant in 1869, captain in 1870, chief of the Detective Bureau in 1883. Byrnes established an office in the stock exchange with telephone connections to every bank in lower Manhattan and boasted to the Roosevelt Committee that from March 12, 1880, on, "they have not lost a ten cent stamp in Wall Street by a professional thief; not a penny, not a cent."

Likewise in the Fire Department, the Irish rose to prominence. From the 1830s to the 1860s, before the city had established a Fire Department, the volunteer fire companies were the spoils of ward politics, and they had many Irish firefighters. When the city finally established the Fire Department, organizers drew many of its appointed firemen from the ranks of the volunteer companies. Two-thirds of the one hundred firemen killed between 1865 and 1905 in New York City were of Irish descent, reflecting the high percentage of Irish firemen. Of the firefighters lost in the World Trade Center

attack on September 11, 2001, roughly one-third were of Irish heritage, demonstrating the ethnic group's continuing dominance in the department.

In the rapidly expanding infrastructure of New York City, young and strong Irish lads found ample work in the construction trades. As construction moved northward and infiltrated the surrounding counties of the city, Irish laborers excavated tunnels, built bridges, dug foundations, laid brick walls, and created a labyrinth of cobblestone streets. Large construction projects came to Irish contractors, and laborers, under the political influence they swayed by their voting blocks.

Ironically, the creation of Central Park offered the Irish ample work while at the same time it displaced a large number of the "shanty" Irish, who lived in Seneca Village. The settlement was an integrated community of 264 immigrant Irish Americans and freed African Americans, who, along with their

(Above) Portrait sketch of inspector Thomas Byrnes (Opposite left) Fireman on duty. (Opposite right) Thomas Byrnes gives the crook the "Third Degree."

On Post.

(Drawn by C. DE GRIMM, by permission of Mr. JAMES GORDON BENNETT.)

pigs, goats, and other animals, were essentially rendered homeless for the construction of city's most famous park.

Among the Irish immigrants there are a handful of very successful entrepreneurs that stand out among the rest, primarily because they are so few in number. Daniel Devlin owned

Examining a "Crook."

Devlin & Co., a ready-to-wear garment business. In 1844, financed by his new father-in-law, Luke Corrigan, a wealthy Irish fruit importer, Devlin set up his ready-to-wear and tailoring business. Devlin & Co. was in business for fifty-three years and during its most successful years following the Civil War, Devlin & Co. had three big stores on Broadway, one of which was located at 459 and 461 Broadway, at the corner of Broadway and Grand Street. During the Civil War, Devlin & Co. furnished free uniforms to the nattily dressed Irish Brigade.

Donegal native Charles Knox built his hat business on the basis of a quality hat. Signs advertising his hats were ubiquitous in the 1860s and 1870s. New York's movers and shakers all wore Knox hats. Like other Irish employers, he treated his employees well. His impressive six-

THE LIFE OF A FIREMAN.

story Knox building was located at 212 Broadway on the corner of Fulton Street in lower Manhattan. He manufactured hats at the factory he built in 1840, which was located on St. Mark's Place between Grand Avenue and Prospect Place in the neighborhood of Prospect Heights in Brooklyn. He expanded the factory in 1878, staying in business until the 1950s when men stopped wearing quality hats.

America's first department store was the brainchild of A. T. Stewart, an immigrant born in Lisburn of County Antrim. Stewart opened a department store that bore his name on the east side of Broadway between Chambers and Reade Streets in 1846. He employed the largest number of Irish women in New York City prior to the Civil War. The building that housed his first store was popularly referred to as the

"Marble Palace." It still stands on the northeast corner of Broadway and Chambers Streets, just above City Hall Park. In 1862, Stewart relocated as the carriage trade moved uptown. His "Iron Palace" was located on Broadway between Ninth and Tenth Streets and later became Wannamaker's Department Store. It burned to the ground in 1956.

Starting with the Famine Irish and continuing until the turn of the century, young, penniless "colleens" fresh off the boats flooded the port of New York. Unlike other ethnic immigrants, these young single Irish women came on their own, not as wives or daughters, but as individuals seeking a livelihood. They remained financially focused on their family obligations in the old country. Once in domestic service in New York with room and board provided, most women sent their wages home as "remittances," either in the form of money or tickets for passage. The money these colleens sent home created a phenomenon of "chain immigration" whereby siblings from the old sod could cross the Atlantic in search of a livelihood. If one sister came to New York

and prospered, more often than not other sisters followed looking for work in the city's service industry. A remittance could also provide the means to enlarge the family farm or provide a dowry for a last remaining sister, who then might marry a man with land. In this manner, immigrants helped to alleviate Ireland's land-use problems and reduced its excess population. In a form of global exchange, New York then gained willing and able workers desperate for unskilled labor positions.

The misery and poverty from which the earlier emigrants fled in coffin ships left the first wave of these young women without even rudimentary housekeeping skills or sanitary habits. However, the supply of trained servants could not keep up with the demand from the increasing middle class, a result of the Industrial Revolution. In 1880, an estimated 80 percent of middle-class households had servants, and young single Irish women were in high demand. Nuns functioned as employment agents, giving references as to the honesty and hardworking natures of the young immigrants.

(Opposite) Scene on a New York dock; stevedores on the docks unloading cargo from ships.

SCENE ON A NEW YORK DOCK—STEVEDORES UNLOADING A SHIP.—[DRAWN BY I. P. PRANISHNIKOFF.]

In 1855, an Irish domestic could make between $4 and $7 per month plus room and board in a pleasant neighborhood. Once trained, she was in demand and therefore secure in her employability. In contrast, factory work was exploitive through piecework compensation, physically taxing, and offered unhealthy and dangerous conditions. Furthermore, factory workers barely earned enough money to live in crowded and disease-ridden slums. The Irish servant girls were an enterprising lot and soon were moving laterally between domestic jobs to better their working conditions.

By the end of the nineteenth century, at least 60 percent of the Irish immigrants were single women, coming to America with sisters, friends, cousins, or by themselves.

Despite the odds against them, a few Irish born women became successful entrepreneurs, such as the Switzer sisters, who established an exclusive dressmaking business in the 1870s. Others became grocers, took in boarders once they were married, serviced laundry or worked as seamstresses in their homes.

Most began by organizing at the ladies fairs of their parish churches and then went on to become suffragettes and labor organizers. Many also chose to enter the service of the Church as nuns, and some founded social institutions, such as Sister Irene Fitzgibbon of the Sisters of Charity, who opened New York Foundling Hospital in 1870.

Dispelling the myth that women do not work outside of the home, in 1855 more than 45 percent of the Irish females between the ages of fifteen and forty-nine earned money outside of their residence. Employed as domestics, hotel maids, waitresses, personal servants, housekeepers, nurses, and washerwomen, they represented a sizeable work force. In addition, many also took in boarders as an extra income source.

As rudimentary education became available to Irish children, the first generation of post-immigration Irish American women became typists, stenographers, bookkeepers, clerks, receptionists, secretaries, teachers, and nurses. However, the professional jobs of choice were teachers and nurses, and by

1890, one-third of the city's public school teachers were Irish. Of those who chose the Church as a livelihood, many became parochial school nuns who taught or provided the nursing and administrative staff for the Catholic hospitals.

Among the earliest labor organizers in the country, literally thousands of New York City Irish joined unions in the nineteenth century. Early unions that attracted strong support among the Irish represented the longshoremen, masons, electricians, carpenters, blacksmiths, printers,

EMPLOYMENT OFFICE

shoemakers, and garment workers. Some labor organizations had Catholic names, such as the Knights of St. Crispin, the shoemakers' union. P. J. McGuire, a son of Irish immigrants, grew up on the Lower East Side and became an organizer of the Brotherhood of Carpenters and Joiners. Leonora O'Reilly was an early garment worker organizer and founder of the Women's Trade Union League. Elizabeth Gurley Flynn was an organizer for the Industrial Workers of the World, or "Wobblies," and cofounded the American Civil Liberties Union. Terrence Powderly, an Irish-American from Pennsylvania, was president of the Knights of Labor, which was very active in New York City where 10 percent of its membership was located. He was also active in the Irish nationalist organizations the Clan na Gael, the Irish Land League, and the Ancient Order of the Hibernians.

(Above) New Yorkers seeking Irish immigrant women at the Castle Garden employment office to employ them as domestics in 1866.

h. of Sarony,Major & Knapp, 449 Broadway, N.Y.

for D.T.Valentine's Manu

DEPARTURE OF THE 69TH REGT. N.Y.S.M. TUESDAY APRIL 23D 1861.
THE IRISH HEADQUARTERS AROUND ST PATRICKS CATHEDRAL, COR. PRINCE & MOTT. ST.

Chapter Four

ARCHBISHOP JOHN HUGHES, RELIGIOUS ORDERS, AND PARISH LIFE

When the last Catholic King of England, James I, appointed the first Governor of the Colony of New York, Thomas Dongan (who held office from 1683 to 1688), he sent the colonies their first Irish Catholic dignitary. A few decades earlier, a visiting Jesuit priest reported that one of the two Catholics he found in Manhattan was an Irishman. However, despite these portentous beginnings, in the eighteenth century, the Irish immigrants to New York were primarily Anglican and Presbyterian Protestants from Ulster.

During the eighteenth century and on into the early nineteenth century, English, Spanish, and French Catholics dominat-ed the Roman Catholic Church in New York. However, under the influence of these other European groups, the early Church did not become the cultural icon it subsequently did under nineteenth-century Irish domination. As neighborhood parishes proliferated and swelled with the phenomenal influx of Irish arrivals in the latter half of the nineteenth century, so too did the Catholic Church's prestige and power.

Following the Revolutionary War, less than one percent of Americans were Catholic, and only a few hundred lived in New York City. By 1810, as many as 15,000 of the city's population of 96,000 was estimated to be Catholic, and they were

(Above) Reverend John Hughes, D.D., coadjutor and administrator of the Diocese of New York before he was ordained as bishop and archbishop.
(Opposite) Departure for the Civil War of the Fighting Irish 69th Regiment in 1861, N.Y.S.M., from Old St. Patrick's Cathedral on Mott Street.

predominantly of Irish origin. The ranks of the city's Irish Catholic population steadily increased until the time of the famine, when they exploded. As boatloads of Irish Catholics arrived during and after the great migration of the famine years, they assumed control of the city's Catholic Church hierarchy.

When the Famine Irish arrived in New York City, they found the Church already under the leadership of one of their own. Bishop John Joseph Hughes, then head of the Diocese of New York, had been born into a family of poor tenant farmers in Ireland on June 24, 1797, in Annaloghan of County Tyrone.

At the formative age of fifteen, John Joseph Hughes lost a sister and the family buried her in a local cemetery in Ireland. By British law, the parish priest was forbidden to enter the cemetery and was only able to give the fifteen-year-old Hughes a handful of consecrated earth to sprinkle over his sister's coffin. This experience left a powerful impression on the adolescent Hughes, who sought "a country in which no stigma of inferiority would be impressed on my brow, simply because I professed one creed or another."

At the age of twenty, John Joseph Hughes emigrated to the United States from Annaloghan with his parents to escape the intolerable life of the Irish tenant farmer under the persecution of the British.

With his fierce character forged by British oppression of the Irish Catholics, Bishop Hughes was both revered and feared. A

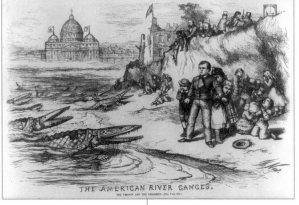

THE AMERICAN RIVER GANGES.

(Above) An anti-Catholic cartoon by Thomas Nast that appeared in *Harper's Weekly* in 1871.
It depicts Catholic priests as crocodile creatures coming ashore to attack the nativist children.

cross preceded his signature, like that of other bishops, but his was in the distinctive shape of a sharp dagger. His followers gave him the nickname "Dagger John" as a sign of respect for his ability to hold the anti-Catholic prejudices in check and never shrink from confrontation. He was the harbinger of the insular Catholic New York community that developed after his death.

Ordained as a priest in 1826, John Joseph Hughes was appointed as an assistant to the then bishop of New York, French-born John DuBois, in 1838. Hughes succeeded DuBois as bishop of New York in 1842 and was appointed Archbishop in 1851 after New York became an archdiocese. He served with great distinction and force until his death in 1864.

Archbishop John Hughes stood up to the anti-Catholic, anti-immigrant, and anti-Irish nativists. He prevented them from terrorizing the Roman Catholic community in New York and burning churches as they did in other American cities during the anti-Catholic riots of 1844. Bishop Hughes had no faith that the city government would protect the Catholic churches and warned the authorities, "If a single Catholic church is burned in New York, the city will become a second Moscow." This was an oblique threat that the city's Protestant churches might burn like Moscow had during the Napoleonic invasion.

Bishop Hughes was a gifted orator and an effective organizer against the nativists. He not only confronted the nativists with his

(Above) Archbishop Bayley of Baltimore imposes the Cardinal's beretta upon Archibishop McCloskey of New York at St. Patrick's Cathedral on April 27, 1875. Cardinal McCloskey became the first American Roman Catholic Cardinal.

37

rhetoric but also recruited 3,000 armed members of the Ancient Order of Hibernians to protect the churches. Never a man to shrink from confrontation, Hughes met with the mayor, Robert Morris, who asked him, "Are you afraid that some of your churches will be burned?" "No sir," responded Bishop Hughes, "but I am afraid that some of yours will be burned. We can protect our own. I come to warn you for your own good." Unlike Philadelphia where St. Michael's and St. Augustine's Roman Catholic Churches were burned to the ground in 1844, not a single church was burned in New York while Hughes was in charge of the diocese.

Bishop Hughes was fully aware of the desperate condition of his newly arrived Irish flock. He understood that the Roman Catholic Church must provide the stability necessary for the Irish immigrants to advance. Before governmental social services were provided, immigrants looked to the Church for guidance, both moral and practical. The ambitious expansionary plans of Bishop Hughes became the aspirations of his flock. Individual responsibility was prodded by the revival of the sacrament of confession. Responsibility was placed squarely on the shoulders of the individual as he intoned, "Forgive me father, for I have sinned." The immigrant Irish Catholics were required to take both personal and collective responsibility for one another.

As the spiritual leader of the Irish immigrants, who were not adequately represented in city government, Archbishop Hughes embarked upon the most expansionary years of the New York Archdiocese. Not only did the Church begin on an ambitious building campaign, culminating in the construction of St. Patrick's Cathedral, but it also expanded its mission, becoming a community center

ST. PATRICKS CATHEDRAL — MOTT ST.

(Above) Old St. Patrick's Cathedral on Mott Street.

with social, recreational, and educational functions to supplement its spiritual authority over the lives of its Irish parishioners. Archbishop Hughes had a temperament suited to the tasks at hand.

Within the Irish Catholic community, far more than other Catholic ethnic groups, the best and the brightest of the immigrant youths aspired to careers in the Church. Having a priest for a son conferred prestige on Irish families. As a result, the Irish have dominated the hierarchy of the Archdiocese of New York ever since. Eleven of the twelve bishops and archbishops have been Irish, namely Bishops Conanen and Connolly, and Archbishops Hughes, McCloskey, Corrigan, Farley, Hayes, Spellman, Cooke, O'Connor, and Egan. Beginning with Archbishop McCloskey, each successive archbishop has been named a cardinal. Five of Brooklyn's seven bishops have been Irish.

Many Irish men and women took holy orders. The women chose among the Sisters of Mercy, Sisters of the Good Shepherd, Dominican Sisters, Sisters of Charity, and Josephite Sisters. For men the choices were the Franciscan Brothers, Fathers of Mercy, Pallottines, Passionists, Redemptionists, and Vincentians. Each of these religious orders was a predominantly Irish order. They provided the staff necessary for Catholic churches, schools, hospitals, orphanages, and old age homes.

Archbishop Hughes helped to develop a strong Irish Catholic communal responsibility through these churches, parochial schools, fraternal organizations, and religious orders. His New York Irish flock fulfilled his vision of a united and powerful Irish community able to move from abject poverty to the middle class in one generation. The funds necessary to realize this came not only from church collection plates,

(Above) St. Mary's Roman Catholic Church on Grand Street.

ST. PATRICK'S ROMAN CATHOLIC CATHEDRAL, FIFTH AVENUE, BETWEEN FIFTIETH AND FIFTY-FIRST STREETS, NEW YORK.

VIEW OF THE INTERIOR OF THE MAGNIFICENT EDIFICE ON THE OCCASION OF THE OPENING OF THE GRAND FAIR OF THE ROMAN CATHOLIC CHURCHES OF NEW YORK CITY, OCTOBER 25th, 1878.—FROM SKETCHES BY OUR SPECIAL ARTIST.

but also from the efforts of the women of the parishes, who turned their handiwork into cash for the church by holding grand church fairs every other year in each parish. With the Church counseling its parishioners to wait to marry, the large population of single Irish women, unfettered by husbands and children, had the time to devote to massive organizational efforts. This freedom from family responsibilities enabled them to mount successful fundraising efforts through the fairs that raised 40 percent of the budget for various parishes. The final completion funds for the new St. Patrick's Cathedral came from the great forty-two-day fair held in the nave of the new cathedral.

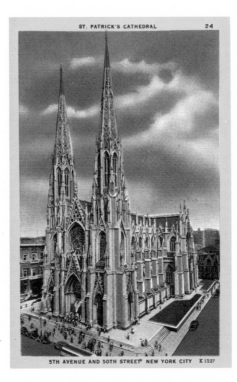

ST. PATRICK'S CATHEDRAL   24

5TH AVENUE AND 50TH STREET, NEW YORK CITY   K 1227

Ladies' fairs were a major social event for a parish, but by no means the only one. Some of the city parishes had eleven or more social events a year, including dances, drama clubs, minstrel shows, card parties, and picnics.

When Bishop Hughes was first appointed, there were six principal Catholic parishes, all of which were predominantly Irish. They included St. Peter's at 22 Barclay Street on the corner of Church Street, St. Mary's at 44 Grand Street on the Lower East Side, Old St. Patrick's at 262 Mott Street on the corner of Prince Street, St. Joseph at 365 Sixth Avenue in Greenwich Village, and two churches in what is now Chinatown, Transfiguration at 25 Mott Street and St. James at 32 St. James Street.

(Above) St. Patrick's Cathedral (Opposite) The Grand Fair in St. Patrick's Cathedral to raise funds for its completion.

Hughes created a massive bricks and mortar campaign that ensured more parishes for more Irish Catholics. By the 1860s, the archdiocese had thirty-one churches, forty-three schools, two hospitals, and three new cemeteries: Calvary in Woodside, Queens; Holy Cross in East Flatbush, Brooklyn; and Mount Olivet in Maspeth, Queens. By the 1870s there were roughly two hundred Catholic churches and chapels in the city and the numbers of parishioners swelled, as their social class improved. In the nineteenth century, between 40 and 50 percent of the people in Irish neighborhoods belonged to a local parish, and by the early twentieth century the percentage had increased to 70 percent.

Hughes deplored the proselytizing by Protestants among the sick and dying in the city's Protestant hospitals. Catholic hospitals were necessary to allow the dying to hear last rites. To this end, St. Vincent's Hospital opened on 13th Street between Third and Fourth Avenues in 1849. It was staffed by Irish nuns from the Sisters of Charity led by Mary Angela Hughes, administrator, nun and sister of John Joseph Hughes. In 1865, the Sisters of the Poor St. Francis founded St. Francis Hospital in what is now New York's Lower East Side.

Under the expansionary program begun by Archbishop Hughes, the Catholics had facilities to take care of their own through a new community infrastructure of Irish aid societies,

(Above) Bishop Charles E. McDonnell and Reverend Thomas Malloy with a group of Brooklyn Dioceses priests vacationing in Eastern Long Island in 1912. Father Malloy (right) succeeded Bishop McDonnell in 1922. (Opposite) St. Patrick's Cathedral on Fifth Avenue, 1878.

churches, parish schools, colleges and universities, hospitals, orphanages, and cemeteries. No longer were the Irish dependent on Protestants for essential services.

The Draft Riots of 1863 occurred seven months prior to Archbishop Hughes's death. On Sunday, June 12, 1863, the newspapers published the names of those drafted through the lottery held the day before. In reaction to the unfair impact of the draft, a mob numbering an estimated 50,000 people, many of whom were Irish immigrants, rampaged through the city for three days. Five days after the riots started, although he was ill at the time, Archbishop Hughes spoke to crowds from his balcony in favor of the northern states, calming the crowd.

When he died, Hughes was no longer at odds with city government. According him the respect he had demanded for his flock, the City Council ordered all municipal offices closed and the flags flown at half-mast. More than 100,000 people gathered outside old St. Patrick's Cathedral for his funeral.

Hughes did not live to see his dream of a new St. Patrick's Cathedral realized. The site of the new cathedral that Hughes chose was located at the far northern edge of the city on a site that had been purchased by church trustees in 1810 for a cemetery. At that time the city stretched only as far north as 23rd Street, but as the city grew around it, its location between 50th and 51st Streets on Fifth Avenue became midtown. The project cost four million dollars and took fifteen years to

complete. The architects James Renwick and William Rodrique, who was married to Archbishop Hughes' sister Margaret, designed the soaring cathedral. Hughes laid the cornerstone in 1858 and expected to consecrate the new cathedral in 1867. However, construction was halted during the Civil War and was later resumed by his successor, Cardinal John McCloskey, who dedicated St. Patrick's on May 25, 1879.

St. Patrick's Cathedral remains the preeminent symbol of Irish Catholic New York. A major attraction to tourists and New Yorkers alike, it stands as a monument to John Joseph Hughes, New York's spiritual and practical leader of his predominantly immigrant flock. The

(Above) A painting of St. Brigid's Church at Avenue B and Ninth Street by Dave McCutcheon, 2005. St. Brigid's was dedicated in 1848 to victims of the Irish Famine.

body of Archbishop Hughes was removed from old St. Patrick's to the new cathedral, where he lies interred under the altar. After completion of the new St. Patrick's, city organizers changed the route of the St. Patrick's Day parade to Fifth Avenue. It is from the steps of St. Patrick's Cathedral that the archbishop greets the St. Patrick's Day parade each year. St. Patrick's is the eleventh largest church in the world. Its French Gothic marble and granite towers rise 330 feet above the street. It has a length of 398 feet and a breadth of 174 feet, and seats approximately 2,400 people.

For all of the modern day disaffection with the Catholic Church, for the Irish, Catholicism is so culturally ingrained that even those who have drifted away from the Church remain tied to it. In *Tin Wife*, Joe Flaherty presents two characters talking about religious affiliation. One says, "I'm a Catholic, you know." The other answers, "Well, we all are, I guess. I mean, even if we don't practice like we used to, it's always there. It's like your mother. I mean, if you don't get on with her, she's still your mother."

In 1992 the Irish rock star Sinéad O'Connor, appearing on *Saturday Night Live*, ripped up a photograph of Pope John Paul II to show her anger with the teachings of the Roman Catholic Church. A few years later, in a backhanded compliment, she apologized to the Holy Father, and an apostate priest in Ireland ordained her. New York's Irish community looked on her antics for the most part with condemnation, although a minority sympathized with her.

(Above) St. Peter's Roman Catholic Church at Barclay and Church Street, the oldest parish in the city.

Chapter Five

RECLAIMING LITERACY:

The Advent of the Parochial Schools

"Build the schoolhouse first and the church afterward."

—Archbishop John Hughes

From highly educated Jesuit priests to rudimentarily schooled blue-collar workers, the Irish are a literate people. The Irish reputation as superb storytellers is now legendary, and when ethnic stereotypes abounded, the Irish were said to have the "gift of gab." Ireland is the country that produced the poet William Butler Yeats, the playwright John Synge, and the novelist James Joyce. Irish tradition is, in short, a literate one carried on today in New York City by Frank and Malachy McCourt, Jimmy Breslin, Maureen Dowd,

Anna Quindlen, Peggy Noonan, and Pete Hamill. Considering that English was considered a second language in Ireland and that most of the population remained uneducated due to the Penal Laws, the Irish have overcome great odds to be such a literate people.

Under the Kilkenny statutes and the Irish Penal Laws imposed by the British, for decades it was against the law to use Gaelic. The restrictive laws also forbade the education of Irish Catholics for nearly two centuries. In the face of the harsh Penal Laws, Irish schoolmasters held classes outdoors to avoid severe reprisals against any person harboring a school. They held open-

(Above) A father reluctantly turns over his two young children to a nun at St. John's Home for destitute boys, established by the Roman Catholic Orphan Asylum and staffed by the Sisters of Charity, c. 1890s. (Opposite) The 2004 Commencement in front of Keating Hall, Fordham University.

air sessions commonly called "hedge schools" within the shelter of hedges, grassy banks, and ditches to hide teachers and their pupils where they could disperse if the British authorities approached. Learning was considered a seditious activity, yet it was not uncommon to encounter a trilingual farmer, accomplished in Latin, Greek, and Gaelic.

Only the Irish love of learning can explain how their passion for education and other cultural expressions endured in spite of every effort to thwart it, in both the old country and the new. Indeed, despite the horrific living conditions of the Famine Irish in Five Points, they managed to become, and remain, literate enough to rise to the middle class within a generation or two of their arrival upon American shores.

Bishop Hughes made education central to his plan for the redemption of his immigrant flock and he was a champion of parochial schools. Hughes said, "In our age the question of education is the question of the Church."

In 1800, St. Peter's, the oldest Catholic parish in New York State (dating from 1785), started the first Catholic school in New York, St. Peter's Free School. In 1805, the state legislature began to subsidize the Free School Society in New York City to defray the cost of educating children. Catholic children had to endure many hardships as the hands of insensitive "educators," who referred to them derogatorily as "papists." Teachers included anti-Catholic and anti-Irish history and literature, and the Protestant King James Bible became the overriding book of choice in each classroom. Bishop Hughes was appalled by the proselytizing of Catholic youths and he demanded that state funding be provided for Catholic education, just as it was for Protestant education.

(Above) Malachy and Frank McCourt, outside New York's Museum of Natural History, October 13, 1998.

With hopes of finding decent educational opportunities for their children, Irish Catholics sought other institutions where they might find a more hospitable climate. Officiates laid the cornerstone of old St. Patrick's Cathedral on May 14, 1809, and dedicated the Church on May 14, 1815. By 1817, administrators opened the St. Patrick's parish school. Old St. Patrick's served as the seat of the Archdiocese of New York until the dedication of the new St. Patrick's Cathedral on May 25, 1879.

By 1839 the Public School Society had eighty-six schools that received public funds, while the seven Catholic schools garnered no assistance. In 1841, reacting to the refusal of both Democratic and Whig political parties to change the school funding arrangement, Bishop Hughes called a meeting in Carroll Hall. He then formed a Catholic political party with the hopes of putting forward a slate of candidates for the State Assembly. Not a single candidate running on the Catholic ticket, called the "Carroll Hall Slate," won, but the new party split the Democratic vote and three Whigs from the city were elected. Tammany Hall, the Democratic political organization with an increasing Irish constituency, was duly alarmed and successfully sought a compromise with Hughes. In 1842, the New York State Legislature passed, and Governor William H. Seward signed, the Maclay Law setting up a new Board of Education in New York City, which prohibited the teaching of any specific religious doctrine.

✢ ✢ ✢ ✢ ✢ ✢ ✢

Mid-nineteenth-century official estimates of the number of homeless children in New York City ranged from 15,000 to 40,000. Street children lived by their wits and survived on the edge of society. They earned money shining shoes, sweeping the streets, selling newspapers, corn, flowers, neckties, matches, and cigars. Some worked as street musicians singing or playing an instrument for donations. Empty spaces between buildings or under stairs, hidden spots in alleyways or under the bushes in parks, all provided sleeping quarters. In the winter they slept on steam gratings or broke into basements or storage rooms for shelter.

Charles Loring Brace, a Protestant from Connecticut who moved to New York City in 1848, wrote: "As Christian men we cannot look upon this great multitude of unhappy, deserted, and degraded boys and girls without feeling our responsibility to God for them." A reformer, his first measure was to start the Children's Aid Society, an orphanage, to provide a safe place for vagrant children to sleep and eat.

Brace then implemented a radical plan for solving the street children problem. He gathered homeless "orphans" and shipped them off to families in upstate New York or in the West. He called it the Emigration Plan. Between 1854 and 1929, a quarter of a million children, many from New York City, were sent to live with rural families. About half the children were sent by the Children's Aid Society and the rest by other charity groups.

Almost all the receiving families were Protestant and the vast majority of the children in this deportation program were Irish Catholics. Not all were orphans. Some were from one-parent families or had simply been part of a street round up. New York City's population was almost half Catholic by the Civil War, and the Catholics were at the bottom of the economic scale. The Catholic Church strenuously opposed Orphan Trains, and Archbishop John Hughes viewed the program as a plot to kidnap Catholic children and turn them into Protestants. For Hughes the objection was that the Orphan Trains were a Protestant operation that preyed on Irish Catholic children. Some found good homes, but others were exploited for their labor as unpaid farm hands and domestics.

The New York Foundling Hospital, a Roman Catholic institution operated by the Sisters of Charity of Saint Vincent de Paul, started its own emigration program for infants in 1870. The infants sent away, however, had been left anonymously at the doorstep of the Foundling Hospital. Catholic parish priests had notified most of the rural or small town adopting families, and the children went to Catholic homes.

Archbishop Hughes sought to ensure that Catholic orphans were brought up in the Catholic religion. To this end he formed

The Society for the Protection of Destitute Children, known as the "Catholic Protectory." It was funded primarily by Catholic donations but also had a modicum of city and state funding. Hughes oversaw the conversion of a 114-acre farm in Westchester into orphanage facilities with a mission to provide Catholic religious instruction and to teach the children useful trades.

The Annual Report of the Police Justices for the year ending November 24, 1884, notes that there were 665 persons sent to the Roman Catholic Protectory, out of a total of 2,671 persons claiming to be destitute. That same year, 554 were sent by the Jus-

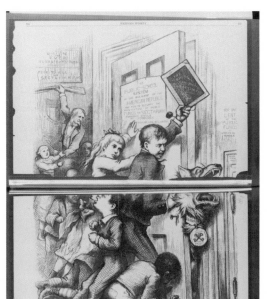

tices to the Mission of the Immaculate Virgin; 283 to the Juvenile Asylum; 237 to St. Joseph's Asylum; 200 to the Institute of Mercy; 150 to the House of Refuge (New York's juvenile reform school); and 29 to the Home of the Good Shepherd.

In New York City, the educational goal of Archbishop Hughes was to open a grammar school in every parish. His plan ultimately succeeded and the parochial school system of the Roman Catholic Church, dominated through much of its history by Irish priests and nuns, educated thousands of New Yorkers.

The Latin School, organized by educators in 1801, was not only New

(Above) Students at St. Cecilia's School in Greenpoint (1910). The parish was founded in 1871 in Greenpoint.

(Above) St. Joseph's School on Pacific Street, Prospect Heights, taken in 1914. The school was staffed by the Franciscan Brothers.

York City's first Roman Catholic school, but it was also located in the first parish of the city, St. Peter's. Later in the mid-nineteenth century under Hughes, the number of parochial schools increased at an exponential rate. At the time of Hughes's death the New York Archdiocese operated forty-three schools around the city. By 1900 half the parishes in New York City had parochial schools, enrolling approximately one-third of the city's Catholic youngsters. Parochial education peaked in the 1950s with about 40 percent of Catholic children attending the Church's elementary schools and one-quarter enrolled in parochial high schools.

In 1841, Bishop Hughes had asked a group of Jesuits, who were working in Kentucky at the time, to come to New York and start a school. Bishop Hughes wanted the school's location to be in Rose Hill, now a part of the Bronx. The Jesuits made good on their word and established St. John's College, the predecessor to what is now Fordham University. The Jesuits also wanted an institution in the center of the city, and in 1847, they created the Manhattan branch of Fordham in an area adjacent to Five Points

at the corner of Elizabeth and Walker Streets. During its first year, a fire temporarily forced the fledgling school into the basement of nearby St. James. Fordham later relocated twice more, leasing space in the East Village, until administrators ordered the construction of a permanent institution at 15th Street off 6th Avenue. In 1861 the school on 15th Street was independently chartered under the name of the College of St. Francis Xavier. However, the Jesuits of both St. Francis Xavier and Fordham maintained close ties for many years hence. In 1913, the College of St. Francis Xavier closed and Xavier High School opened at the 15th Street location. Fordham became a university, but it did not return to Manhattan until it opened a campus as part of the Lincoln Square Renewal Project.

Under the guidance of the archdiocese, Catholic religious orders opened many other high schools and colleges in New York City, including Fordham University, Saint Joseph's College, St. John's University, Mount Saint Vincent's College, Manhattan College, Marymount Manhattan College, St. Francis College, and a number of Catholic high schools.

In 1907, the Institute of the Religious of the Sacred Heart of Mary founded Marymount College, a Catholic women's college in Tarrytown, New York. The original order established its first community in Ireland. While Marymount College of Tarrytown and Fordham University consolidated in 2002, Marymount Manhattan College remains an independent institution, offering an excellent education to women. Women such as Marymount's founder, Mother Joseph Butler, educated young Catholic women for positions of leadership, and many former students went on to become teachers themselves.

As the Irish Catholics moved from the city into Long Island, Westchester, and New Jersey, they left an educational legacy in their parochial schools. Transfiguration, the parochial school situated in the middle of what was once the notorious Five Points neighborhood, is now located in Chinatown. Its student population is more than 90 percent Chinese. In a city where public schools are constantly criticized for their lack of excellence, the parochial schools quietly go about the business of educating immigrants from Asia and South America, fulfilling their original purpose, although no longer exclusively for the Irish.

(Above) Faculty members at Bishop McDonnell Memorial High School. The faculty was composed of members of a variety of orders, including Sisters of Mercy, Sisters of St. Joseph, Sisters of Charity, and Sisters of St. Dominic.

St.Pat, Parade '09   670-13

Chapter Six

THE ST. PATRICK'S DAY PARADE:

1 7 6 2   t o   t h e   P r e s e n t

St. Patrick is most often depicted with his crosier in hand, driving the snakes out of Ireland. The snakes symbolize the demons expelled from Ireland by St. Patrick. After the expulsion, legend has it that Ireland was free of evil for seven years. Ironically, St. Patrick was not Irish.

What is known of St. Patrick's life is more legend than fact. He was born in 387 A.D. into the family of a high-ranking Roman official living in Briton, then a Roman colony, and first came to Ireland as a captive slave named Paticius. When he was sixteen, Irish invaders

captured Patrick in a raid on his family's estate and took him to Eíre to work as a slave tending sheep among the Druids and other pagans. During his years as a slave, he absorbed the Irish culture and Celtic language. He then managed to escape back to Briton, where he reunited with his family and studied for the priesthood with the help of a cleric who may have been his mother's brother, St. Martin of Tours. After his ordination as a bishop, Patrick returned to Ireland in 433 A.D. with a dual mission of ministering to the Christians already living in Ireland and

(Above) A 69th Infantry recruitment poster, 1917. (Opposite) St. Patrick's Day Parade, 1909.

converting others to the faith. While converting the assembled chieftains at the Féis of Tara, Patrick plucked a shamrock from the ground, using it to explain the Trinity. The shamrock remains the symbol most commonly associated with the Irish and the St. Patrick's Day Parade.

Every year on March 17—unless March 17th is a Sunday, and then it is delayed one day—the Irish celebrate their patron saint's day with a parade up Fifth Avenue. The Archbishop of New York greets the parade from the steps of St. Patrick's Cathedral. The parade route is from 42nd Street up Fifth Avenue to 86th Street. New York's parade is the largest and the oldest consecutive annual St. Patrick's Day Parade in the world. Even Dublin's parade dates back only to the 1990s.

The St. Patrick's Day Parade is the only large parade in New York City that is without floats or other vehicles of any kind, except for the occasional baby stroller. It also boasts no amplified music. It is a marching parade, a show of solidarity with the Irish and a display of Irish nationalism. What began as a show of

THE APOSTLE OF IRELAND ST. PATRICK, BORN A.D. 372, DIED A.D. 4
Serpentes et omnia venenata animalia ex Hibernia baculo suo expulit.

strength to the Orangemen has become an occasion to honor and support the city's Irish heritage. The marchers from the Police Department and Fire Department, once predominantly Irish, now include many ethnicities that proudly march in uniform with the Irish.

A small group of Irish soldiers in the service of the British Crown on March 17, 1762, marched to John Marshall's Inn, located at Mount Pleasant, near what was then known as Kings College, later renamed Columbia College. They were the first to commemorate St. Patrick's Day with a march in New York City. This small march was the first in a succession of annual parades that have continued from that day to the present.

The military originally organized the parade, but after the War of 1812, Irish fraternal and benevolent societies took over. These included the Friendly Sons of St. Patrick, an Irish Protestant organization, and the Ancient Order of the Hibernians (A.O.H.). In 1851 planners designated the A.O.H as organizer, and the group named a Grand Marshal as the titular head of the parade. Traditionally, members of the A.O.H., the Grand Marshal, and members of the Parade Committee start the celebration of St. Patrick's Day by attending Mass at St. Patrick's Cathedral.

As native Protestants became progressively more aggressive toward Irish Catholics, and the Famine Irish arrived, the parade became a show of force in defiant opposition to the nativists.

(Above) By 1872, St. Patrick's Day was marked as a proud day-long celebration of Irish heritage. (Opposite) A Currier & Ives print of St. Patrick with crosier and a snake.

By the Civil War, the parade included 10,000 marchers, most of them the Famine Irish. It visually demonstrated the growing number of Irish Americans, their political clout, and their support of Irish nationalism. Finally, after Irish Catholics had come into their own in city government, the parade became a celebration of Irish heritage and Irish nationalism.

The A.O.H. has its roots in a parent organization with a 300-year history in Ireland before congregants at St. James Church established the North American A.O.H. on May 4, 1836. The initial purpose of the group was to protect Catholics and their churches from attacks by the anti-Catholic "Know Nothings." It is the largest and oldest Catholic lay organization in the United States and restricts its membership to practicing Roman Catholic men, aged sixteen years or older, who are either Irish immigrants or descendents of Irish immigrants.

For the Irish, unlike other immigrants, the Roman Catholic Church is not only a separate institution from the state but historically represents outright opposition to the hostile ruling authorities. Perhaps this is why the St. Patrick's Day Parade has supported Irish nationalism so strongly over the years and is sponsored so vigorously by the A.O.H.

In 1853, the Know Nothings, under the leadership of Bill Poole, attacked members of the A.O.H. who were marching in the Independence Day Parade. Aggressors drove a team of horses and a wagon into A.O.H. marchers and

Erin go bragh!

(Above left) Postcard: lass with harp flag (Above right) A political button supporting the prisoners in Long Kesh, the Irish prison where Irish political prisoners are held.

fighting broke out, resulting in injuries to a number of Irish marchers. The threatening nature of the Know Nothing attack on the priorInde-pen-dence Day was the impetus behind an unusually large military escort for the following St. Patrick's Day Parade in March 1854. In keeping with the tradition started when the nativists posed a threat, a military unit leads the parade even today.

Year after year the parade has grown as more Irish arrive in America. The parade now includes more than 150,000 marchers and an estimated one to three and a half million spectators. Recently, organizers have welcomed an overwhelming number of groups, including the 165th Infantry, the successor to the Fighting Irish 69th, more than 400 parochial, high school, and college marching bands, fife and drum corps, bagpipers, Irish county and benevolent societies, the police, the firefighters, the 42nd Infantry with their Irish wolfhounds, Irish step dancers, Irish fraternal organizations, women's auxiliary organizations, and other associations.

The A.O.H. approved the display of Irish nationalism in support of the Hunger Strikers of H Block in Northern Ireland's Long Kesh prison in the 1982 St. Patrick's Day Parade. The display recalled a long, proud history of support for Irish nationalism, echoing the Celtic origins of a proud defiant people, not always violent in their persuasive techniques.

(Above) Marchers at the St. Patrick's Day Parade, 1920.

The A.O.H. support for Irish nationalism does not mean that the St. Patrick's Day Parade is necessarily open to other forms of political activism by Irish marchers. With the support of the state courts and the Second Circuit Court of Appeals, the A.O.H. has reserved the power to exclude the Irish Gay and Lesbian Organization (IGLO) from the St. Patrick's Day Parade. The A.O.H. parade rules prevent any group or person from using the parade as a vehicle or forum to pursue any political, social, or commercial agenda inconsistent with the message, values, and viewpoint of the A.O.H. Any potential marchers with a particular purpose, principles, or agenda inconsistent with the teachings of the Roman Catholic Church will not be allowed to march. Among those denied the right to march in the past by the Parade Committee were the Right-To-Life Organization and the Budweiser team of horses.

The symbolism of the parade is mixed, but at its core is respect for the Irish, who have made such monumental contri-

(Above and right) St. Patrick's Day Parade's traditional bagpipe bands on March 17, 2005.

Irish community of the city, the parade represents their dual allegiance to their ancestral land and their new world lives. The parade is no longer exclusively Irish. It now welcomes people of many ethnicities, marching within other groups, such as the police, firefighters, parochial schools, and high school bands. The parade is the largest civilian parade in the world and traditionally all New York politicians march. On St. Patrick's Day in the city of New York, it is often said that everyone is Irish.

butions to the great city of New York. Some of the Irish deplore the drunken revelry that St. Patrick's Parade has come to represent. Others look to the day to provide a sense of their culture. The Holy Name Societies, the parochial schools, the county societies, and the school bands represent a family, social and religious values.

The St. Patrick's Day parades celebrates the incredible contribution that the Irish have made to the social, political, economic, and religious fabric of New York City. And to many in the

(Above left) Step dancers in traditional costumes, March 17, 2005. (Above right) St. Patrick's Day Parade, March 17, 2005.

Chapter Seven

TAMMANY HALL:

Patronage, Scoundrels, and Reformers

Native Protestants originally formed The Society of Saint Tammany as a patriotic organization and social club in 1786 with the object of protecting the young republic. Middle-class professionals and artisans created the society in opposition to the elite men's clubs of the upper classes from which they were excluded. Like the Masons, the society had a secret order laden with rituals and symbolism. The founders had titled their new club after a legendary Delaware Native American Chief, whose name was variously written as Tamany, Tamanen, Tamaned, Taming, and Teinane. His admirers in the Revolutionary War era mythologized him as "St. Tammany, the Patron Saint of America." Members called their meeting hall a "wigwam" and during gatherings donned Native American costumes, applied war paint, brandished tomahawks, marched "single-file Indian style," and passed a peace pipe. While the Native American pageantry lasted only until the 1820s, the nomenclature endured. The use of the word "Saint" in the title, originally added by the nativists to give offense to the "papists," was dropped, as more of the immigrant Irish became members. Eventually, with the steam

(Above) Tammany Hall, situated on 14th Street, east of Union Square. (Opposite) John F. Kennedy at Gracie Mansion, May 20, 1962.

provided by the burgeoning ranks of Irish party regulars, the Tammany Society machine evolved into a political machine, allying itself with the Democratic Party.

Tammany Hall organized its records by moons and seasons. The society had thirteen tribes, the number of original states and the number of Indian moons that marked the passage of time in each year. Each of the tribes had a leader called a "sachem," and the head of the society was called the "Grand Sachem" or "kitchi okeemaw." The wild Bengal tiger (popularized by the famous political cartoonist, Thomas Nast, as a symbol of Tammany Hall) was the symbol of the Americus Engine Company, a company of volunteer firemen called Fire Company No. 6. One of those volunteer firemen, William M. Tweed, became a famous Tammany Hall politician, known as "Boss" Tweed. In 1860 society members elected the first Irish Catholic Grand Sachem, James Conner. William M. Tweed sponsored Conner, despite the fact that Tweed himself was a Protestant of uncertain ethnic background.

(Above) Tammany Hall provided such colorful material that it inspired a melodrama dramatizing the excesses of the Tammany politicians.

The Irish had arrived in America with a conflict-driven sense of community. For centuries before the arrival of the Famine Irish in America, the Catholic Irish had banded together to oppose the British and the Protestant Irish. In New York City, Archbishop Hughes helped them to flex their nascent political muscle. Hughes tried to use his clout and influence at Tammany Hall from the very beginning by demanding that public funds be used for parochial schools. The archbishop lost this first battle, but in the process received a valuable political lesson regarding voting and constituencies. His flock began to vote in solid blocks through ward bosses, and the immigrant Irish soon became the power behind Tammany Hall by virtue of their ever-increasing numbers. By 1844, an estimated ninety percent of Irish Catholics voted Democratic.

THE TIGER'S SHARE
Tammany—"I'm monarch of all I survey;
My right there is none to dispute.
From Harlem right down to the bay

Tammany's power was grounded in political favors. In the poor immigrant neighborhoods, the Irish residents swapped votes for social services at a time when city government offered none. If a widow needed a bucket of coal or a returned Civil War veteran needed a job, Tammany would oblige. Favors meant votes, but even so, reforms were slow in coming.

The rise of Tammany Hall's political influence, and the scope of its graft and corruption, must be understood in an economic context. From 1850 to 1900, the city's population increased from 600,000 in Manhattan and an additional 200,000 people in adjacent Brooklyn, to 3,437,202 in a five-borough city. The city moved northward at a dizzying pace, with new buildings advancing its boundaries almost weekly. The city issued a staggering number of construction permits and undertook large

(Above) *The Tiger's Share*, a cartoon by H. Gillam, using the tiger symbol of Tammany Hall to depict the influence of Tammany Hall on the city. This was one of the many political cartoons instrumental in instigating the scathing exposé of the corruption of Tammany's control of the city government.

public works projects in response to the demands of the growing population. It was in this political and economic environment that the Irish found a place for themselves, moving up to the middle class in one or two generations. As the city grew, civil service jobs increased exponentially under Tammany Hall patronage, and many of the positions went to the Irish. These were the halcyon days for the New York City Irish, who had a lock on City Hall and enjoyed the benefits of its patronage and nepotism.

The insecure Famine Irish craved the stability provided by the new civil service positions. In response to the demand for increased services, the city government created new civil service agencies, and the Irish stood first in line for the new positions. Many of the Irish volunteer firemen became civil servants in 1865 when the city folded the volunteer fire companies into the Metropolitan Fire Department. The Police Department went from a total of 1,846 men when the new Municipal Police Act went into full effect on August 1, 1845, to 7,426 in 1900. The Department of Street Cleaning became the new sanitation agency in 1872. The composition of the Fire, Police, and Sanitation Departments, and, in the following generation, the Board of Education, reflected the new political clout of the Irish.

The urban public works projects required a large number of unskilled laborers. By preceding the arrival of later waves of Italian, German, and Jewish immigrants, the Irish beat them to most of the jobs in the building trades. The Irish were the work force that strung the electric lines above ground, and then moved them below ground. They were the laborers who built Central Park and the new Tweed Courthouse, constructed and extensively renovated several times by the Tammany politicians. The Brooklyn Bridge, completed in 1883, was also a product of Tammany Hall patronage. Completed under the direction of the Irish-born contractor William Kingsley, the fourteen-year bridge project employed many Irish laborers, skilled and unskilled.

New York City politicians became masters at practicing graft and corruption, aided in large part by the ever-increasing urban population. George Washington Plunkett, an Irish Tammany politician, said, "I seen my opportunities and I took 'em." He also distinguished "honest graft" from other forms of political skullduggery. Plunkett explained how he became a millionaire through the system he manipulated so well: "Well, I'm tipped off, say, that they're going to lay out a new park at a certain place. I see my opportunity and I take it. I go to that place and I buy up all the land I can in a neighborhood. Then the board of this or that makes its particular plan public, and there is a rush to get my land, which nobody cared particular for before. Ain't it perfectly honest to charge a good price and make a profit on my investment and foresight? Of course it is. Well, that's honest graft."

As the Irish-born immigrant population of New York City increased, so did the power of Tammany Hall. The Tammany influence helped the new immigrants not only find jobs and housing, but attain citizenship in return for their votes. Not surprisingly, by mid-century, the Irish vote was dominant. This in turn concentrated the power in the hands of the Tammany Grand Sachem, Boss Tweed. Tammany leaders that succeeded Boss Tweed included several Irish Americans, most notably, Honest John Kelly, Richard Croker, Big Tim Sullivan, and John F. Curry. Under their leadership, Tammany Hall was still synonymous with graft and corruption, but also respected as an extremely effective political machine. The newspapers increased their satirical exposé of the Tammany abuses, with cartoonist Thomas Nast responsible in large part for the inevitable movement from within Tammany for reform.

(Above) Portrait of Richard Croker, leader of Tammany Hall from 1886 until 1901.

It is abuses and excesses that inspire reform. Tammany Hall exploited the patronage of city government at a time when, due to a conjunction of economic circumstances, the city could actually afford to hemorrhage money to the Tammany politicians. For many years the greed and corruption of the Tammany politicians knew no bounds. Boss Tweed built and remodeled his new Tweed Courthouse at a cost of $13,000,000, a staggering sum in the nineteenth century. These costly renovations are now exhibited in tours of the Tweed Courthouse, which still stands behind City Hall in City Hall Park. Eventually, however, under the guidance of Charles Francis Murphy, the thrust of Tammany politics gradually began to change from a political machine aimed only at increasing its own sphere of influence to a political force for reform through Al Smith.

The political ascendancy of Al Smith (1873–1944) was a Tammany success story. Raised in the old neighborhood of Five Points and serving as an acolyte in his local parish, he left parochial school in the parish of St. James at the age of twelve to support his family. He became friends with two leaders rising in the Tammany ranks, Tom Foley and Henry Campbell, and landed a job serving subpoenas. He moved up in the Tammany ranks and soon ran for political office, serving in the state legislature from 1903 to 1915. Although Al Smith himself was never a sachem of Tammany, he was clearly its spokesman. He became governor of the State of New York, serving from 1918 to 1920 and again from 1922 to 1924, and represented the progressive wing of Tammany Hall. He advocated in the State Legislature for rent regulation, workers'

(Above) Mr. and Mrs. Alfred E. Smith leaving St. Patrick's Cathedral on Easter, 1941.

compensation, and public housing. In 1928, he was the Democratic candidate for president of the United States, losing to Herbert Hoover. Anti-Catholic sentiment was credited with his poor electoral showing. Although New York would send Daniel Patrick Moynihan and James Buckley to the U.S. Senate, and Hugh Carey, born and raised in Brooklyn, to the Governor's Mansion, it would not be until 1961 that the Irish Catholics would have a man in the White House, John Fitzgerald Kennedy.

Ironically, it was the penchant for reform from within Tammany that gave rise to the transformation that would eventually weaken Tammany. In reaction to the newspapers' clamor against the excesses and abuses of Tammany, the city undertook an investigation led by Judge Samuel

Seabury. The Seabury investigations resulted in the resignation of Tammany Mayor Jimmy Walker on September 1, 1932. In December 1932, Al Smith voluntarily appeared before Judge Seabury to explain his plan for the comprehensive reform of Tammany politics through changes in the New York City charter. Although an Albany legislative committee killed Smith's plan under the direction of the still powerful Tammany politicians and their allies, another anti-Tammany politician, Mayor Fiorello La Guardia, eventually carried out charter reform in 1936. The Tammany tiger wounded by rehabilitation, survived until the mid-twentieth century. Gradually, Tammany lost its Irish Catholic leadership, as the Irish left the ranks of the city political regulars and moved out to the suburbs.

(Above) Senator Daniel Patrick Moynihan at his favorite bar, McGoverns, on Eighth Avenue. Photo by William Coupon.

Chapter Eight
SLÁINTE: TO YOUR HEALTH

Wine comes in the mouth,
And love comes in at the eye.
That's all we shall know for truth
Before we grow old and die.
I lift the glass to my mouth
I look at you and I sigh.

"A Drinking Song"
—W. B. Yeats (1865–1939)

The Irish love of drink is a cultural stereotype and a near mystical experience for the American Irish. Many Irish youths come of age believing that drinking to excess is an essential part of their Irish American identity. Irish American playwright Eugene O'Neill's play, *A Long Day's Journey*

into Night, is an autobiographical exploration of this dark side of Irish culture. Likewise, Pete Hamill's book, *A Drinking Life,* chronicles this aspect of the Irish character. Only recently have prominent Irish American New Yorkers Frank McCourt and Hamill challenged this heritage by daring to be sober Irish writers.

Excessive alcohol consumption is an American overlay to what it means to be Irish. It is only in America that the Irish identity is entwined with drink. In *Irish America: Coming into Clover,* Maureen Dezell explores the Irish reputation as a hard-drinking lot and reveals along the way that Ireland is respectably

(Above) Eugene O'Neill in Northport, Long Island, summer 1931. (Opposite) McSorley's Old Ale House at 15 East 7th Street.

behind France in its per capita consumption of alcohol.

In nineteenth-century New York, liquor establishments served as political clubs and employment agencies for Irish immigrants, as well as a place for communal lamentation of their sorry lot. In 1850, the neighborhood of Five Points had a liquor purveyor for every sixty residents, and bosses paid Irish laborers in part with rotgut whiskey to discourage unrest. One of Thomas Nast's anti-Irish cartoons, published in 1872 in *Harper's Weekly*, depicts an Irish mother bent over with children and a drunken husband on her back.

Like Roman Catholic parish churches and parochial schools, Irish

(Above) *Pot Bellies (McSorley's)* by Gregory de la Haba, 2002.

pubs assumed an important social role in Irish American culture. Drinking with the lads was a recognizable cultural phenomenon. Male camaraderie found in the pubs substituted for familial life among young Irishmen, who waited until they could support a family before starting one.

Adhering to the legacy of the past, St. Patrick's Day celebrations are rarely dry, and drunken and disorderly behavior among the parade-goers is expected. Traditionally, the St. Patrick's Day celebration starts at early Mass, but many Irish New Yorkers begin their observance with breakfast in a midtown Irish bar. The combination of food with green beer and Irish whiskey is not an uncommon one.

Irishmen commonly distilled alcohol illicitly during the 1700s and early 1800s in the rural areas of Ireland. Peasants produced *poteen*, a crudely distilled whiskey with a fiery palate, in reaction to the repressive laws and corrupt British authorities. For the newly arrived Famine Irish in the slums of New York City, the rotgut whiskey sold in grocery stores and taverns replicated the mind-numbing experience that poteen had provided in Ireland.

The oldest continuously operated drinking establishment in New York City is the famous Irish bar McSorley's Old Ale House, located at 15 East Seventh Street near Astor Place. John McSorley founded the bar before the Civil War in 1854, and his son, Bill McSorley, ran the bar from approximately 1890 until he sold it in 1936 to Daniel O'Connell, a policeman, who promised to make no changes. The original name was the Old House at Home, which the owners changed to McSorley's Old Ale House in 1908

after the sign blew down. Founder John McSorley drank steadily from age twenty until he was fifty-five, when he gave it up, but his son Bill never indulged in the habit.

Many politicians used McSorley's as their hangout, and with protection from his regulars, Bill McSorley continued to openly serve liquor throughout the era of Prohibition. It has remained a favorite bar to many generations of serious drinkers. In August 1970, it finally opened its doors to women in compliance with the "McSorley's Law," named for the bar, which prohibits discrimination in public places. Before the passage of the law, if a woman passed through its front door, bar employees rang a bell hanging over the front door to signal male patrons to begin booing loudly.

McSorley's retains much of its original character by refusing to change its décor. The bar still has the potbellied stove and sawdust covered floors made famous by John Sloan's paintings completed between 1912 and 1930 and by the Bernice Abbott photograph of its interior. For an historic review of the bar's first eighty-eight years, "The Old House at Home" is a 1940 short story by Joseph Mitchell, in his book *The Old Hotel*, as part of a set of stories about McSorley's entitled *McSorley's Wonderful Saloon*. More recently, the artist Gregory de la Haba has done a series of paintings reminiscent of the earlier Sloan paintings. A bartender of many years at McSorley's, de la Haba is married to the first and only woman bartender at McSorley's, Teresa Maher de la Haba, daughter of the current proprietor, Matthew (Matty) Maher. Another of McSorley's barkeeps, Geoffrey Bartholomew, has been working behind the bar since 1972, and he has used the kaleidoscope of McSorley's imagery as his poetic muse. Bartholomew published an entire volume of poetry inspired by McSorley's in 2001, entitled, *The McSorley Poems*.

During Prohibition from 1919 to 1933, many Irish bars closed their doors. But when the dry era was over, bars like the Landmark Tavern on the far West Side, which opened in 1868, P. J. Clarke's (opened in 1894), and Peter McManus, a fourth-generation family-owned business in continuous operation since 1936, once again thrived. Other Irish New York bars, still in operation but of more recent vintage, include Manhattan's Jack Dempsey's, Moran's, O'Hanlon's, O'Neal's, The Scratcher, Tír na nÓg, Annie Moore's, Connolly's, and Rosie O'Grady's. A few of the formerly ubiquitous Blarney Rose bars sprinkled throughout the city still survive as well. Blarney Stone is in Midtown, Blarney Star is near City Hall, and the Kilarney Rose is in the Financial District. These are dark, well-worn establishments for a regular to slip into for a bite to eat and a pint before, during, or after work.

In Brooklyn, the most picturesque and historic of the old Irish bars is Farrell's, located off Bartel Pritchard's Square in Windsor Terrace. The Windsor Terrace area was once an almost exclusively Irish neighborhood populated by civil servants, many of whom had summer homes on the "Irish Riviera" in Far Rockaway. Park Slope has Mooney's Pub and O'Connors; Brooklyn Heights has O'Keefe's and Eamon Doran's; and Bay Ridge has Peggy

(Opposite) Poetry and folk singing at McSorley's, 1959. Photo by Burt Glinn.

O'Neill's. In the Bronx, Fieldston has Dorney & Malone's Tavern; Woodlawn has Mulligan's Pub; Staten Island has Bridget's in West Brighton.

Queens boasts the largest number of operating Irish bars outside of Manhattan. Jackson Heights has Legends Bar; Astoria has McLoughlin's; Flushing has McGriskin's Pub; Woodside has Kilmegan's and Riordan's; Sunnyside has Easy Street; Long Island City has P. J. Leahy's and Shannon Pot; and Broad Channel has its Grassy Point Bar and Grill. Many of the bars sponsor softball teams, dart leagues, and some even support horseshoe leagues. Irish music sets at some are always a good draw for the music-loving Irish.

Pete Hamill summed up the lure of the Irish bar in *A Drinking Life*, saying, "The culture of drink endures because it offers so many rewards: confidence for the shy, clarity for the uncertain, solace to the wounded and lonely, and above all, the elusive promises of friendship and love."

(Above and Opposite) Colorful Irish pubs in New York City.

© 1915. Brucker & Co. Photo by Brucker & Co. N.Y.

Chapter Nine

SOCIAL IDENTITY AND RECREATION:

Organizations, Sports, Music, and Dance

ORGANIZATIONS

The first of the New York Irish societies was the Friendly Sons of St. Patrick, formed in 1784 by Protestant Irish New Yorkers. With the influx of poor Roman Catholic immigrants during the last half of the nineteenth century, Irish-American societies began to proliferate with a variety of religious, social, and political agendas. Some were religious, such as the Holy Name Society, some were fraternal, like the Ancient Order of the Hibernians, and some were formed for military purposes,

including the Fermanagh Republican Guards and the Limerick Guards.

The political organizations included both Irish nationalist and American organizations formed to provide patronage and better working conditions. There were also benevolent societies such as the Donegal Relief Fund, created to provide relief to the famine-stricken parts of Donegal. Others were ladies' aid societies, and a few were simply social. As the immigrants adjusted to American life, the various county, political, and religious societies formed an Irish subculture within the city.

(Above) Membership certificate in the North American Ancient Order of Hibernians, 1894. (Opposite) The Emerald Ball held at the Waldorf Hotel ballroom in 1916. This charity ball was first held in 1839, and holds the distinction of being the oldest consecutive annual charitable ball in New York City.

An effort by the Irish to knit the various county societies together was sparked by their desire to match, if not exceed, the accomplishment of the German American community's social centers. To this end, in May 1897, members of the Irish Volunteers, an organization of independent Irish military companies and Clan na Gael held a month-long Irish Fair at the Grand Central Palace located at Lexington Avenue and 43rd Street. The fair served as a fundraiser for the Irish Palace Building Association, an organization formed to finance, build, and manage an Irish hall that would function as a club to which every Irish person would belong. The plans included a library, riding school, and shooting range.

The centerpiece of the Irish Fair was a huge topographical map of Ireland spread out across the floor and inlaid with the outline of the Irish counties, each filled with soil certified as to its county of

origin. Standing on the hallowed ground of their home county precipitated many tearful, emotional displays from the sentimental Irish, who never thought they would walk on Irish soil again. As a fundraiser, the map was a rousing success at 10 cents admission. A contemporary newspaper, *The Irish World*, reported that "For the price of ten cents one can tramp all over Ireland." The money raised was donated to the American Irish Historical Society for the purchase of the building at 991 Fifth Avenue that is still used by the society today.

The county societies are primarily social organizations today. Each year the county societies proudly bear their banners for the full length of the St. Patrick's Day Parade. Ties to Irish home counties are still held dear. Irish Americans, several generations removed, still query one another about their family's county of origin.

(Above) The façade of the American Irish Historical Society on Fifth Avenue.

Ironically, the various counties finally came together in an enduring organizational structure during the late nineteenth century, not in cooperation but rather in competition, through the Gaelic Games. The county societies organized a sports team network. Hurling and football, competitive sports, finally linked the counties together in a durable relationship. In the 1890s there were a number of well-known Irish teams. Most of the teams were named for Irish patriots or given other Irish nationalistic names, and only one was named for a county, the Kilkenny Football Team, organized in 1898. As the counties began to field teams of their own over the next few years, the Kickhams, whose members were all from Tipperary, simply switched their name in 1904 to the Tipperary Football Team.

Private Irish promoters finally made playing fields permanent with the acquisition of Celtic Park in 1897. Celtic Park was a nine-acre athletic field located in Laurel Hill, a neighborhood in Queens close to Calvary Cemetery, known then as the "City of the Celtic Dead." With public transportation expanding, Celtic Park and Calvary Cemetery were accessible and became a common destination for the Irish after Mass on Sundays. After a visit to the cemetery, the afternoon was free for picnics and games in the park.

In 1897 the Irish American Athletic Club (IAAC) was formed, and its members began to train at Celtic Park. Many IAAC members were famous athletes. Martin Sheridan from County Mayo won five Olympic events and set sixteen world records in various field sports. Eight out of the thirteen American wins at the 1908 Olympics in London were by members of the IAAC.

(Above) Ladies Football—The Annie Kearney Cup, Mayo vs. Na Fianna, July 11, 2004, Gaelic Park.

The Irish Counties Athletic Union (ICAU) made schedules and organized the matches between the county teams without county favoritism; eventually purchasing a rival park in the Wakefield neighborhood in the Bronx. Unfortunately, hopes for the success of Wakefield Park were dashed by several factors, including the Blue Laws preventing the ICAU from charging admission fees to sporting events held on Sundays and its remote location. The park was forced to close soon after it opened. Despite the failure of Wakefield Park, the ICAU, later renamed the United Irish Counties, survived, and by 1930, clubs representing all thirty-two Irish counties were affiliates.

Celtic Park was finally eclipsed by the relocation of the Gaelic Games in 1928 to Innisfail Park. Celtic Park itself was redeveloped into residential housing apartments after it was sold to a developer following the First World War.

Innisfail Park, purchased by the Gaelic Athletic Association of Greater New York (GAA) in 1926, is situated on the north side of 240th Street and west of Broadway in the Bronx, close to Manhattan College. After being run by the GAA for about ten years, it was acquired by the city. The property was then leased to John "Kerry" O'Donnell, who ran the park, dance hall, and bar with the help of an extended network of family and friends. In deference to the GAA's contributions, it was renamed Gaelic Park in the 1950s. Manhattan College became steward of the park in 1991, and it is now known as the Gaelic Park Sports Center. The college uses the facility for several sports including its home games of soccer, lacrosse, and softball.

From 1914 to 1976, the GAA organized the Gaelic Games. The Gaelic Games continued to be played at Gaelic Park until

(Above) The Paddy Markham Cup, Co. Clare cs. New York Senior Football in Gaelic Park, April 23, 2005. (Opposite) Celtic Park, Dublin Jr. Football Team, c. 1930.

...BLIN Jr. Football Team Celtic Park Aug 17 1930. O. McCoy Capt.

the GAA transferred the games to Fordham University in the Bronx.

Another venue for Irish games is the Rockland County Feis and Field Games, sponsored by the Ancient Order of the Hibernians. Since the first festival in the 1970s, this annual event has attracted thousands of Irish American New Yorkers and others to watch Irish football, hurling, and sheaf throwing, listen to modern and traditional bands, including 50 pipe bands and 300 individual pipers, buy imported linen, crystal, and jewelry from Ireland, and participate in dance, music, song, art projects, and a soda bread bake-off.

MUSIC AND DANCE

In their centuries' long struggle for cultural autonomy from the British Crown, the Irish miraculously kept the coals of their music and dance traditions alive, dancing at the cross-roads and even below the decks of the coffin ships to the tune of an Irish fiddler. Nevertheless, many of the Irish musicians who immigrated to New York during the 1920s found it impossible to make a decent living from their music because their fellow immigrants took their cues from Irish Americans who wanted to fit in, and assimilation did not allow ethnic cultural expression. Still, they found outlets for their music.

During the twenties and thirties many talented and popular Irish musicians played at various events throughout the city, including céilis, dances, and feís. These venues paid little, however, and it was necessary to earn an income as a musician through whatever paying venues were available. Certain dance halls became popular meeting places for the Irish community on weekends

(Above) Press box at Gaelic Park in the Bronx.

and provided jobs for musicians, but only if they played more popular forms of music.

The Irish community was blessed with incredibly talented musicians such as Larry Redican (fiddler), Hugh Gillespie (fiddler), James Morrison (fiddler), Tom Ennis (piper), Neil Nolan (tenor banjo), Dan Sullivan (vocals), Murty Rabbet (vocals), John McGettigan (vocals), and the Flanagan Brothers (vocals), who preserved the traditional forms of Irish music as well as created impressive new tunes and lyrics. They reminded many nostalgic immigrants of their homeland across the ocean.

During the 1940s and 1950s, several circumstances in America conspired to stamp out traditional forms of artistic expression by groups from foreign cultures. The era of Big Band music and the House Un-American Activities Committee both contributed to the suppression of nonnative voices. Radio and subsequently television rigidly defined cultural preferences in American music and dance, including the big band sound and the foxtrot.

Despite their public show of being "American," in musical tastes, the Irish, having been psychologically conditioned by centuries of British repression, were able to keep their traditional music alive in private sessions, variously termed "home parties" or seisúns. These sessions, generally held in private homes, often lasted into the wee hours of the night. These were reminiscent of centuries of seisúns around the cottage peat fires of Ireland.

In 1950 the formation of Comhaltas Ceoltóirí (Association of Irish Musicians) in Ireland signaled the beginning of the first of the now hugely popular All-Ireland Fleadhs. For each annual Fleadhs, the best Irish traditional musicians flung worldwide by

(Above) The Chieftains.

the diaspora and their progeny return to Ireland to compete against one another for music championships. Irish music had begun its revival in Ireland, but it took another decade for the American Irish to publicly support their music. For America, it took both the resurgence of immigration from Ireland in the 1950s and the 1960s revival of folk music as a popular music form to popularize Irish music.

During the sixties folk era, skilled musicians, who previously played only in private homes and at seisúns, could perform once again in public venues. The Clancy Brothers and Tommy Makem was a band formed in New York after the brothers and Makem had separately emigrated from Ireland in the 1960s. The band popularized Irish music with their energetic, audience-pleasing performances. They started in the coffee houses of Greenwich Village, the center of the folk music revival, and went on to produce more than fifty albums. The Clancy Brothers and Tommy Makem were influential in the commercial success of the

Lawrence, Publisher, Dublin.

THE OULD IRISH JIG.

"Then a fig for the new fashioned waltzes
Imported from Spain and from France,
And a fig for the thing called to polka,
Our own Irish jig we will dance."

Dubliners, a group, which followed suit in Dublin. The Clancy Brothers and Tommy Makem paved the way for later more serious traditional Irish musicians to recapture the minds and hearts of Irish Americans, such as the Chieftains and Sean O'Riada's group, Ceoltoriri Cualann.

In need of new source material, the folk musicians of the 1960s looked to the past, and Irish poems and ballads were increasingly incorporated into the repertoire of musicians featured at Village clubs. One such successful pairing of verse with song is the recording of William Butler Yeats' *Down by the Salley Gardens* by such artists as Tommy Makem, Liam Clancy, Clannad, Maura O'Connell, and many others. The producers of *Dancing at Lughnasa*, a film based on Brian Friel's play by the same name, included the song in their movie as arranged by Bill Whelan and sung by Dolores Keane.

Other well-known American performers, such as Peter, Paul and Mary, delved into the rich legacy of Irish poetry to create memorable music. One such tune is "Shule Aroon," adapted from an old Gaelic poem:

> *I would I were on yonder hill,*
> *'Tis there I'd sit and cry my fill,*
> *and every tear would turn a mill*
> *Johnny's gone for a soldier. . . .*

The name of the poet is lost to history, but the piece was saved for posterity by its publication in a book that Yeats edited, *A Book of Irish Verse*, an anthology first published in 1900.

The Chieftains, a traditional Irish music group that has produced thirty successful albums, themselves built on the advance work of more popular songs in the repertoire of The Clancy Brothers and Tommy Makem. While the groups are at two different ends of the folk music spectrum, they each represent a side of Irish culture that has its roots in Yeats' concept of "Irishry." This richness of the Irish musical tradition may be the result of the compression of all of Irish Catholic Gaelic society into one class under British domination, which forced the Irish to combine high and low culture. As a result, Irish literature, poetry, lyrics, and music are imbued with both classical and hedge school

(Opposite) "The Ould Irish Jig."

influences. This universal cultural appeal is apparent in the Irish traditional music that has recently become so popular among Irish Americans. The Chieftans and The Clancy Brothers enjoy a tremendous popularity, as do newer additions to the music scene, such as U2, Mary Black, and Sinead O'Connor.

Since the sixties, Irish music has been well received in North America, with New York as the premier venue. In 1969, The Wolfe Tones, an Irish group, came to New York to open Bill Fuller's Old Shieling Hotel. They received good press and enjoyed great success in the United States, where they have been touring for two months a year for the past thirty-five years. Other bands formed in the 1970s, Planxty, the Bothy Band, and De Dannon, have likewise been well received when playing in New York.

By the eighties, New York's music scene had evolved sufficiently to birth some local Irish music groups itself, such as Altan. During this era, musician Mick Maloney organized the group Cherish the Ladies, named for a jig of the same name. Cherish the Ladies, based in New York City, consists of all-female musicians who perform with step dancers. The band garnered support from the National Endowment for the Arts and the Ethnic Folk Arts Center to create a kick-off concert series. Under the strong leadership of the Irish-American Joanie Madden, born in Brooklyn, who plays flute, whistles, and sings harmony vocals, Cherish the Ladies has enjoyed a vibrant presence for more than sixteen years. In 2002, the BBC named the ensemble Best Musical Group of the Year, and it was also named

(Above) Tommy Makem and The Clancy Brothers, 1960s.

the Entertainment Group of the Year by the *Irish Voice* newspaper. One of the original members of Cherish the Ladies, Bronx native Eileen Ivers (a fiddler), has gone on to produce her own albums, which, in keeping with the musical times, fuses her Irish music with other ethnic rhythms.

In the 1990s and early twenty-first century, sensitivity to various forms of ethnic music emerged in response to exposure to the many channels on the television and the simultaneous popularity of many different forms of music in various media forms, CDs, mp3 players, and Internet radio from around the world. Various radio broadcasts, including those of RTE (an Irish radio station) and the Thistle and Shamrock weekly radio show in New York, have exposed many Irish Americans to their musical roots and expanded the audience for Irish traditional

music. In addition, various music festivals, such as the annual Feis Nua Eabhrac ar Oileain Staten (New York Festival in Staten Island) on the grounds of the Snug Harbor Cultural Center, have expanded the audience for all forms of Irish music.

Ethnic fusion defines the current cultural state of affairs in all music forms and Irish music is no exception. Examples include a New York Irish-American rock band, Black 47, named after the worst year of the Famine, which enjoys a rising popularity with nine albums to their credit. In addition to straight music, the group has a political agenda, writing songs that address, among other issues, unrest in Northern Ireland. Gael Force, also based in New York, creates a unique sound by mixing droning bagpipes, electric fiddle, and mandolins with rock band instrumentation. In the nineties, Solas was formed. It

(Above) Cherish The Ladies, an Irish traditional music ensemble.

includes a New Yorker, Winifred Horan, on fiddle, and Susan McKeown, a Dublin-born vocalist who relocated to the East Village. Like many contemporary groups, Solas draws on unusual source material, such as the writings of Emily Dickinson and Samuel Taylor Coleridge.

New York is home of the premier Irish music label, Shanachie, which musicologist Richard Nevins and musician Dan Collins started out of a Bronx apartment in 1975. What began as a modest venture to release and promote a small number of traditional Irish records has since mushroomed, and the company is now expanding into other ethnic source material.

The city also hosts a number of Irish music programs on the Fordham University radio station, WFUV, including "A Thousand Welcomes," a language arts show on Saturdays, "Ceol na nGael" (the Music of the Irish) on Sundays, and the popular "Thistle and Shamrock" Irish music program. In 1974, two Fordham students, Gerry Murphy and Mary McGuire started the first of these programs and currently the listening audience for the station's Sunday afternoon menu is almost 75,000 people.

The Irish brought their love of dance to the city as well. The mingling of immigrants and the American-born Irish at dance halls, as well as at seisúns in the early part of the twentieth century standardized the set dancing, which is in style somewhat like American square dancing.

In Ireland, the various set dances required intricate footwork, all particular to the locality in which they originated. Step dancing, as a form of solo dancing, first appeared at the end of the eighteenth century. At that time in Ireland, wandering dance masters went from village to village, each teaching within his district. Contests between dance masters at fairs were common. From this past came a rich dance legacy.

Today in New York City, soft shoe and hard shoe (hornpipe) step dances, céilí dances, and set dances have attained great popularity. Céilí dancing is patterned group folk dancing done in lines, circles, or squares with names like the Cross Reel, Eight-

Hand Jig, and Stack of Barley. Set dances, a precursor to American folk dances, are more complex than céilí, although their titles are equally colorful: Ballinascarty Half Set, Fermanagh Quadrilles, and Corofin Plain. Colorful traditional costumes on male and female dancers with Celtic detailing are an important complement to the intricate footwork.

The mid-1990s saw the birth of two major Irish dance companies. Irish choreographer and dance master Michael Flatley created the

artistically and commercially successful *Riverdance* and then went on to present *Lord of the Dance*. Both of these dance shows have enjoyed tremendous international popularity. Wonderful musicians such as composer Bill Whelan and Eileen Ivers were involved in the formation of *Riverdance* and helped contribute to its success. Bill Whelan won a Grammy Award for Best Musical Show Album in 1997 for his original music and lyrics for *Riverdance*. Step dancing has found new life, and many groups integrate the form into a variety of Irish musical performances everywhere.

Irish culture transplanted in New York, as expressed through its county societies, sporting events, and the arts, has proven to be indestructible, despite its shift from agrarian to urban environment. New York, as a vital center of Irish culture, has both preserved and strengthened the sense of community, while adding its own original contributions to what it means to be Irish.

(Above) A scene from *Riverdance*, featuring lead dancers Melissa Convery and Irish-born, New York raised, Padraic Moyles, 2004.

· IRISH FREE STATE ·
HOSPITALS' SWEEPSTAKE TICKET

NDER THE PUBLIC HOSPITALS ACT 1933.
MMITTEE UNDER THE CHAIRMANSHIP

CONDUCTED AND MANAGED BY THE HOSPITALS
OF VISCOUNT POWERSCOURT

NATIONAL

RUN AT
INTREE, ENGLAND
MARCH 19TH 1937

PRIZES ON REVERSE

UNDER THE SUPERVISION
COMMISSIONER OF POLICE
N MARCH 15TH 1937

USINESS HOUSE
ND IN IRISH FREE
YOUR COMMUNI
TO US

ERS:
UST LTD.
TERRACE,
F.S.

IMPORTANT THAT
LF REGARDING THE
THE TRANSMITTER. IF
UNREQUESTED, SEND
TO IRISH FREE STATE.

EVERY PRIZEWINNER WILL
BE NOTIFIED OFFICIALLY

MAKE SURE TICKETS, COVERS OF BOOKS AND
RECEIPTS SHOW WATERMARKED IN THE
PAPER THE WORDS
"SWIFT BROOK LTD. IRELAND MADE $1000
REWARD CONVICTION IMITATORS"

J McGrath
MANAGING DIRECTOR

SUBSCRIPTION
10/-

JP 160170

TEN SHILLINGS
STERLING

LEADING TO CONVICTION OF PERSONS

$1000 REWARD FOR INFORMATION

COUNTERFEITING THESE TICKETS

Chapter Ten

TIES TO EÍRE ENDURE

Generation after generation of Irish New Yorkers remain tied to Mother Ireland. Centuries of reaction to harsh British repression inoculated many Irish immigrants against total assimilation. No other cultural influences have been able to replace their quintessential Irish character. Passionately attached to America as well as to Ireland, the Irish maintain a dual citizenship of the soul.

Whether it was the location of a poteen still or a hedgerow school, the Irish stood in solidarity against the anti-Catholic and anti-Irish sentiments of the Britons and, in their adopted country, against those sentiments of the nativists. These traits served them well in New York City and kept them ethnically centered as they formed tight networks through parish churches, fraternal organizations, and ladies' aid societies.

The bonds tying the city's Irish American community together are the same that bind Irish Americans to Ireland itself. Roman Catholicism, the St. Patrick's Day Parade, Irish traditional music, storytelling, ancient Gaelic games, the ethos of the Irish family, and, above all else, Irish nationalism, continue to link the Irish-Americans to their origins. The unwelcome reception upon their arrival in

(Above) Funds for the Republic of Ireland were raised in New York by the sale of bonds. By its inscription, this bond is to bear interest "from the first day of the seventh month after the freeing of the territory of the Republic of Ireland from Britain's military control." The bond is dated November 15, 1921, and is signed by Eamon de Valera, as President of the Republic of Ireland. De Valera was a first generation Irish American born in New York City. (Opposite) An Irish sweepstake ticket, March 19, 1937.

America by the nativists only served to strengthen their ties to one another and to Ireland.

As New York City expanded exponentially during the last quarter of the nineteenth century, Irish Americans benefited directly from this boom and finally began to enjoy relative economic prosperity. Their acceptance in the Democratic political organization, the advent of union activity, and the flourishing social, sports, and educational endeavors indicated more leisure time for the Irish. Instead of focusing this energy on their immediate families, the unmarried, energetic young immigrants looked back to their home and became ardent Irish nationalists united around the single-minded focus of freeing Ireland from British rule.

Tales of Irish generosity during famine times and in steerage during the long journey to America are legendary. Individuals shared what they had with those in need and placed importance on not "getting above yourself." Irish American civil servants used their influence to secure work for friends and relations, as

(Above) The Cuba Five, named for the ship on which all five Fenians pictured here were released to America. They sailed for New York on January 5, 1871. From the left: John Devoy, Charles Underwood O'Connell, Harry Mulleda, Jeremiah O'Donovan Rossa, and John McClure.

did those in construction and other industries, thus creating economic security for all. The narrow economic and social differentiation among the Irish immigrants, as they all moved up into the middle class together, strengthened their ties to one another and to Ireland.

Money flowed back across the Atlantic from New York to aid relatives, provide relief to the general Catholic population in Ireland, and further Irish political causes. Ireland's economic reversal in the late 1880s sent another wave of Irish immigrants to New York. These newcomers, fresh from the Land Wars, served as a catalyst within the City's Irish community to stimulate an even greater nationalist feeling.

To this day, politicians and political refugees go back and forth between the Irish communities of New York and Ireland. New York has historically provided asylum to many political refugees from Ireland. In 1858, Michael Dohery and John Mahony formed the Irish Republican Brotherhood, also known as the Fenians, in New York City. Following the Civil War, many U.S. military men moved back to Ireland to give aid to the newly established Brotherhood. Michael Davitt founded The Irish National Land League and Jerome J. Collins, science editor of the *New York Herald*, financially supported the League through Clan na Gael, the Fenian's organization in the United States.

John Devoy, an Irish Republican Brotherhood exile, British prison parolee, and New York immigrant, used his editorship of the *Gaelic American* (the voice of the Clan na Gael) to spread his nationalist message. All Irish Americans rallied to the cause of the Sinn Fein during the 1919–21 Anglo-Irish War. In the 1920s, John DeVoy organized the American Friends of Irish Freedom to sponsor Eamon De

(Above) An 1866 advertisement for Fenian collars contains a portrait of the Irish patriot Robert Emmet.

Valera's 1920 U.S. tour. Eamon De Valera, the first president of the Republic of Ireland, was born to Irish emigrant parents in New York City and frequently moved back and forth between New York and Ireland. Since its inception, Irish Republican Army (IRA) members have often sought asylum in the city.

Irish New Yorkers followed the news of their homeland through several newspapers, among them were *Gaelic America*, *Irish America*, *Irish Advocate*, and *The Irish Echo*. First published in 1859, *The Irish Echo*, is still available weekly. More recently, immigrants use the Internet for news, which provides them with full and immediate access to all Irish events, including the Gaelic Games. They can also watch the Games on cable channels accessed through satellite connections.

The Irish have often returned to their native land, paying heed to the land. President Kennedy, in appreciation of the Irish Catholic vote, soon after his election made a triumphant visit to Ireland in 1961. Following his lead, as air travel became more affordable, Irish Americans went "home" to reaffirm their roots. The air traffic between New York and Ireland has increased over the years. For many, visiting Ireland serves as a counterbalance to the multicultural bombardment of New York City.

(Above) Postcard with an Irish flag and inscription: Let Erin Remember.

Despite the great mix of cultures and groups in the city, most of the Irish still center their lives around Irish cultural events, Irish nationalism, and the Church. Irish families make an effort to instill a love of all things Irish in their children. The Irish Arts Center (IAC) located at 553 West 51st Street in Manhattan offers a wide variety of Irish history and cultural arts instruction and celebrations for this purpose. Organizers established the center in 1972, and it still offers Irish theater, dance, music, history, literature, film, and other art forms for students and audiences. The IAC serves as a central location for the preservation of all that is Irish in New York City.

The passion of the New York Irish for their heritage is extreme. Nostalgia for Mother Ireland is passed on to successive generations of Irish American New Yorkers. The lyrics of the sentimental song, "Mother Machree," reflect the strong love for Mother Ireland, as for a mother who has been left behind:

Macushla! Macushla!
Your sweet voice is calling,
Calling me softly,
Again and again,
Macushla! Macushla!
I hear it in vain.

Macushla! Macushla
Your white arms are reaching,
I feel them enfolding,
Caressing me still.
Fling them out from the darkness,
My lost love, Macushla,
Let them find me and bind me
Again if they will.

GLOSSARY

An Gorta Mór (uh GOR-tuh more) "The Great Hunger," was caused by the English land use policies and precipitated by the potato blight, which occurred throughout Ireland between 1845 and 1848.

Blarney is Irish flattery and puffery, with a bit of an untruthful flavor.

Bodhrán is a round frame drum played in Irish traditional music.

Bridget was a name used commonly in a derogatory manner to refer to the Irish female domestic in the late nineteenth century, referring typically to a female servant who is loveable, but ignorant, unskilled Irish girl.

Camogie (Comógaíocht), a Celtic team sport, is the female players' counterpart of the male sport of hurling.

Cead Mile Failte means "100,000 welcomes."

Céili dancing is Irish social dancing that involves large numbers of people.

Clan na Gael was a secret oath-bound society founded for the purpose of liberating Ireland by force.

Donnybrook was a derogatory term coined for a fight involving more than two fighters, intended to indicate that it was an Irish brawl.

Feis is a festival and in Ireland the Feis of Tara dates back to 1300 B.C.

Fenians, also known as the Irish Republican Brotherhood, was formed in 1858 in Dublin and New York as a radical nationalist organization, dedicated to freeing Ireland from British domination by any means necessary.

Fleadh is a music festival.

Hurling is an ancient Celtic game, similar to lacrosse, played on a grassy field with a curved wooden stick made of ash (hurley or caman) and a small hard ball (sliothar). Hurling was played for many centuries in Ireland before the Gaelic Athletic Association standardized the rules in 1884.

Irishry is a term coined by the great Irish poet W. B. Yeats, who used it to denote the quintessential character of the Irish.

Paddy Wagon is an ethnic slur for the wagon that was used to transport those arrested in the latter half of the nineteenth century to the police station or the Tombs.

Poteen is a fiery home-brewed Irish whiskey that gives the imbiber an instant headache.

Seisúns are music sessions either in bars or at other venues where musicians typically jam together.

Set dancing is an Irish dance that involves more intricate steps. Set dances are usually danced by four couples, forming a square, and have evolved from French quadrilles.

Shenanigans are high jinx by the Irish, a sort of mischief.

Shilelagh is an Irish walking stick, often carved, sometimes of Blackthorn.

Sinn Fein is the political organization aligned with the Irish Republican Army.

Step dancing is Irish dancing wherein the dancer's back is straight as a board with arms hanging stiffly down while the feet fly everywhere.

Stout is a deep brown Irish beer, thicker than its pale yellow cousins, which is very filling with a distinctive flavor.

Tír na nÓg is an island situated in legend off the Irish coast, a mythological community where you stay forever young.

(Above) The Irish Arts Center at 553 West 51st Street promotes Irish culture.

LIST OF ILLUSTRATIONS

Page 46: The 2004 commencement, Keating Hall, Fordham University. Courtesy Fordham University

Page 47: At St. John's Home for destitute boys, c. 1890s. Photograph courtesy of Diocese of Brooklyn Archives

Page 48: Malachy and Frank McCourt outside New York's Museum of Natural History, October 13, 1998. Photo: AP/Wide World Photos

Page 51: Thomas Nast. *Tilden's Wolf at Door.* 1876. Wood engraving. Library of Congress, Prints and Photographs Division

Page 52: Students at St. Cecilia's School, 1910. Photograph courtesy of Diocese of Brooklyn Archives

Page 53: Students at St. Joseph's School, 1914. Photograph courtesy of Diocese of Brooklyn Archives

Page 55: Faculty members at Bishop McDonnell Memorial High School. Photograph courtesy of Diocese of Brooklyn Archives

Page 56: St. Patrick's Day Parade in 1909. Library of Congress, Prints and Photographs Division

Page 57: "Enlist To-Day." Lithograph poster. 1917. Library of Congress, Prints and Photographs Division

Page 58: Currier & Ives. St. Patrick with crozier and snake. Lithograph. Library of Congress, Prints and Photographs Division

Page 59: St. Patrick's Day, 1872. Lithograph. Library of Congress, Prints and Photographs Division

Page 60: Vintage postcard and political button. Courtesy of the authors

Page 61 and cover: St. Patrick's Day Parade, 1920. Courtesy Corbis/Bettman

Pages 62–63: St. Patrick's Day Parade, 2005. All photographs by James Casserly

Page 64: John F. Kennedy at Gracie Mansion, May 20, 1962. Courtesy John F. Kennedy Library, Boston

Page 65: Vintage postcard of Tammany Hall. n.d. Courtesy of the authors

Page 66: "A Tammany Tiger." c. 1896. Poster, Library of Congress, Prints and Photographs Division

Page 67: H. Gillam. *The Tiger's Share.* c. 1875. Museum of the City of New York

Page 69: Portrait of Richard Croker. 1901. From *Munsey's* magazine, October 1901. Courtesy of the authors

Page 70: Mr. and Mrs. Alfred E. Smith leaving St. Patrick's Cathedral on Easter, 1941. Museum of the City of New York

Page 71: Senator Daniel Patrick Moynihan at the Landmark Tavern, 1987. Photograph by William Coupon

Page 72: McSorley's Old Ale House, 2005. Photograph by Leslie Jenkins

Page 73: Eugene O'Neill in Northport, Long Island, summer, 1931. Photo courtesy of The Hammerman Collection and eOneill.com

Page 74: Gregory de la Haba. *Pot Bellies* (McSorley's). 2002. Pastel. Courtesy Gregory de la Haba

Page 77: Poetry and folk singing at McSorley's, 1959. Photograph by Burt Glinn. Courtesy Magnum Photos

Pages 78–79: Irish pubs and restaurants in New York, 2005. Photographs by Leslie Jenkins

Page 80: The Emerald Ball at the Waldorf Hotel ballroom, 1916. Photograph courtesy of Diocese of Brooklyn Archives

Page 81: Membership certificate

Page 82: Facade of the American Irish Historical Society. Courtesy American Irish Historical Society

Page 83: Camogie—The Annie Kearney Cup, Mayo vs. Na Fianna in Gaelic Park, July 11, 2004. Photograph by Margaret Purcell

Page 84: Football—The Paddy Markham Cup, Co. Clare vs. New York Senior Football in Gaelic Park, April 23, 2005. Photograph by Margaret Purcell

Page 85: Celtic Park, Dublin Jr. Football Team, c. 1930. Photograph by Larry Luby. Courtesy of the Sunnyside Chamber of Commerce

Page 86: Press box at Gaelic Park, 2005. Photograph by Leslie Jenkins

Page 87: The Chieftains. Photo © James Fraher/Redferns

Page 88: Vintage postcard of "The Ould Irish Jig." n.d. Courtesy of the authors

Page 90: Tommy Makem and The Clancy Brothers, 1960s. Photo © David Redfern, Redferns/Retna Ltd.

Page 91: Cherish The Ladies. Photo by John Francis Bourke

Page 93: A scene from *Riverdance*, featuring lead dancers Melissa Convery and Padraic Moyles, 2004. Photograph by Clarke James Mishler, 2004 © Copyright Abhann Productions

Pages 94–95: Irish ephemera. Courtesy of the authors

Page 96: The "Cuba Five." 1871. Lithograph, Library of Congress, Prints and Photographs Division

Page 97: Advertising circular, 1866. Library of Congress, Prints and Photographs Division

Page 98, 104: Vintage postcards. Courtesy of the authors

Page 101: Façade of the Irish Arts Center on West 51st Street. Courtesy Irish Arts Center

(Above) Crossed Irish and U.S. flags with inscription: "Greetings to Ireland from America's shore; May she live long and prosper, forevermore."

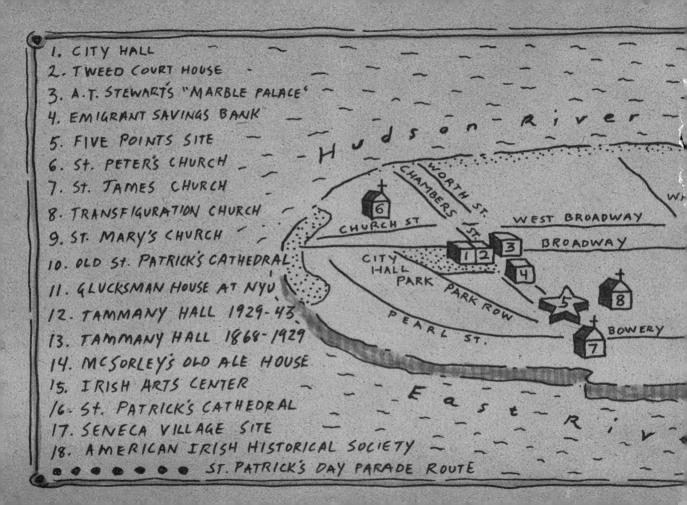

1. CITY HALL
2. TWEED COURT HOUSE
3. A.T. STEWART'S "MARBLE PALACE"
4. EMIGRANT SAVINGS BANK
5. FIVE POINTS SITE
6. St. PETER'S CHURCH
7. St. JAMES CHURCH
8. TRANSFIGURATION CHURCH
9. St. MARY'S CHURCH
10. OLD St. PATRICK'S CATHEDRAL
11. GLUCKSMAN HOUSE AT NYU
12. TAMMANY HALL 1929-43
13. TAMMANY HALL 1868-1929
14. McSORLEY'S OLD ALE HOUSE
15. IRISH ARTS CENTER
16. St. PATRICK'S CATHEDRAL
17. SENECA VILLAGE SITE
18. AMERICAN IRISH HISTORICAL SOCIETY
● ● ● ● ● ● ● St. PATRICK'S DAY PARADE ROUTE

Hudson River

East River

CHAMBERS ST.
WORTH ST.
CHURCH ST
WEST BROADWAY
BROADWAY
CITY HALL PARK
PARK ROW
PEARL ST.
BOWERY